101

Winning
Volleyball Drills

D1514490

Cecile Reynaud

COACHES
CHOICE™

ISBN: 978-1-58518-083-7
Library of Congress Control Number: 2007941732

Book layout: Bean Creek Studio
Cover design: Bean Creek Studio

Coaches Choice
P.O. Box 1828
Monterey, CA 93942
www.coacheschoice.com

Dedication

This book is dedicated to the memory of my parents, Barbara and Jed Reynaud, who supported me throughout my career as an athlete, a student, a teacher, a coach, an administrator, and a clinician.

Acknowledgments

- Thanks to my friends and family members who understand my love of coaching and the game of volleyball.

- A special thanks to my college coaches and mentors, Dr. Mary Jo Winn and Linda Dollar.

- Thanks to Dr. Billie Jo Jones for giving me the opportunity to coach at the collegiate level and continuing to support me throughout my coaching career.

- Many thanks to all my former players and assistant coaches who helped me understand and love the game of volleyball. I appreciated their patience as I matured as a coach.

- Thanks to all the colleagues I have learned so much from at all the clinics I have attended throughout the years and to those of you in the clinics I have taught.

- Finally, thanks to Nancy Marcus for her wisdom and encouragement to go for it throughout the years!

Contents

Diagram Key

LF –   Left front

MF –   Middle front

RF –   Right front

LB –   Left back

MB –   Middle back

RB –   Right back

S –   Setter

MH –   Middle hitter

OH –   Outside hitter

RS –   Right side

B –   Blocker

T –   Target

D –   Defensive player

L –   Libero

P –   Player

W –   Waiting player

C –   Coach

<u>P</u> –   Player on a safe platform

B̲ –   Basket of volleyballs

SB –   Scoreboard

X –   Objects

Moving ball – (dotted line) ……

Player movement – (straight line) _____

Terminology Keys

Antenna: A flexible rod that is attached to the net at each sideline

Attack: The offensive action of hitting the ball

Attack line: A line on each court whose rear edge is three meters (9'10") back from the middle of the center line under the net

Back-row attack: When a back-row player attacks the ball by jumping from behind the attack line before hitting the ball

Block: A defensive play by one or more players meant to deflect a spiked ball back to the hitter's court. It may be a combination of one, two, or three players jumping in front of the opposing attacker and contacting the spiked ball with their hands.

Center line: The boundary that runs directly under the net and divides the court into two equal halves

Cross-court shot: An individual attack directed at an angle from one end of the offensive team's side of the net to the opposite sideline of the defensive team's court

Down ball: A ball the blockers elect not to attempt to block because it has been set too far from the net or the hitter is not under control. This ball is hit overhand and driven over the net with topspin without the player jumping.

Dump: Instead of setting the ball to an attacker the setter sends the ball over the net on the second hit

Endline: The line that extends from one sideline to the other sideline at the end of each court

Free ball: A ball returned by a pass instead of being hit by an attacker jumping at the net

Libero: This individual is a player who only plays in the back row. The libero is restricted within the rules on how and where they can play the volleyball. Check the current governing body rules for specific restrictions.

Line shot: A ball spiked down an opponent's sideline, closest to the hitter and outside the block

Off-speed hit: A ball that is attacked with less than maximum force

Outside hitter: A left-front or right-front attacker

Pancake: A last resort, one-handed defensive technique where the hand is extended and the palm is placed on the floor and timed so that the ball bounces up off the back of the hand

Sideline: A line that extends from one end line to the opposite end line on both sides of the court

Target: A specific area on the court where the ball should be directed

Tipping: An attacker contacts the ball with an open hand off the tips of the fingers

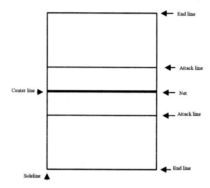

Zones: The court is divided into six areas or zones to denote serving areas, player areas or rotational order. The right back area of the court is known as zone 1, while the right front is zone 2. The numbering system continues around the court, with the middle back of the court known as zone 6.

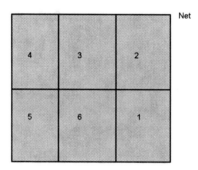

Preface

I had the privilege of coaching women's volleyball at the NCAA Division I level for 26 years. Throughout those years I have had some amazing opportunities to be around fantastic volleyball coaches and players. I have finally compiled a collection of drills for your use. Many I learned from other coaches or I designed them specifically to use with the teams I have coached.

Drills are the individual parts of practice you use to get your athletes to be better players. The ideal way to make them better players is to have them play the game in practice.

It is my hope you will take this book and use the concepts involved to modify these drills for your teams.

Introduction

While this book features a collection of drills, I believe it is also important to cover a few practice concepts. Make sure the activities you use in practice become game-like as quickly as possible. Have a scoreboard available at each practice session to keep track of points scored or lost. It is important to keep score in the drills so players become accountable for their actions and to help them learn how to compete. Use player-initiated drills as much as possible. The better I became as a coach, the less involved I was in running the drill, and the better my team became. Use the net in drills so players get used to the concept of hitting the ball over the net and responding successfully to a volleyball coming over the net. Incorporate consequences for the team, group, or individual who is not successful in the drill. These should be low-impact activities that make the players a little uncomfortable so that they will turn up their competitive level to avoid them. Certain drills in practice are the best time to keep statistics and videotape the activities to help determine starting players. It also gives the non-starting players some valuable information. Implement core-conditioning activities during drink breaks in between drills to make good use of time. Set up drills so they end with a score that will be similar to a final game score, such as 25 or 30 points. Be careful with the number of repetitions you start with. You should adjust the number for your level of players.

Work hard to tell and show your players how to do something correctly, instead of telling them and showing them what they are doing wrong. Talk less and ask more questions of your players, like "What did you see? How did that feel?"

Most importantly, keep the drills fun, but competitive. Drills should be exciting and challenging. Make sure your players experience success in each drill as soon as possible. Players will look forward to practices that get them to work hard and improve. Always have the last part of practice be a six-on-six game of some type. As a result, practice will end on a positive note, and the players will look forward to getting back on the court the next day.

Incorporate practice rules to make the drills run smoothly. Create a positive practice culture. Let your players know some of your pet peeves. For example, I didn't want my team running under the net. If they have a bad pass or dig and shanked the ball, they would have to chase it. I referred to it as "shank and shag." They soon learned to get their body behind the ball.

When you are first teaching volleyball techniques, use basic principles. Set up a demonstration of the skill, give your players a few cues to focus on, let them practice the skill immediately, and coach them with specific feedback to help them improve.

Coaching a team is like cooking something. What you can cook will depend on the ingredients you have to work with. Look at what you have to work with and develop a team that can be successful.

Remember to keep it fun! Players and coaches at all levels want to enjoy their experience in the gym.

1

Warm-Up Drills

Drill #1: Throwing, Catching, and Movement Warm-Up

Objective: To develop correct hitting-arm technique, eye contact with the ball, movement to the ball, and the ability to communicate the player's intention to play the volleyball

Set-up: All players; one volleyball for each set of partners

Description: The players stand across the net from their partner at approximately the attack line. If there are more players than can fit comfortably in the court along the attack line, a rope can be hung up at net height outside the court boundary so the players can throw the ball over an object at net height. Players throw and catch the ball over the net with their partner 10 times in a row, using the correct throwing technique with their serving/hitting arm. When catching the ball, the players should start out calling "mine" as the ball comes toward them. The second set of 10 throws should have the players calling "mine" and watching the ball all the way into their hands to stress "eye contact" with the ball. The third set of 10 throws should have the players calling "mine," "watching the ball" all the way into their hands, and "shuffling into position with the right foot forward" to be directly behind the ball. If the drill is not being done correctly, the count for everyone goes back to zero.

Coaching Point: Coaches should move around on the court, making sure the players are doing the drill properly. This situation is a good opportunity for the coach to stress these simple, but important fundamentals at the beginning of practice. Players should be using a correct throwing motion with the elbow high, calling the ball, watching the ball, and moving to be directly behind the ball with their right foot forward.

Variations: Players can move further back from the net as they get their arms warmed up. They can also move their partners around from side to side or up short and back deep in the court. They should also throw a few balls with their non-dominant hand.

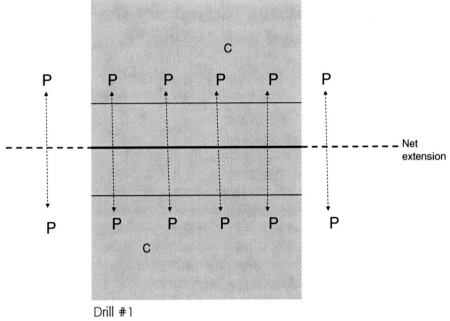

Drill #1

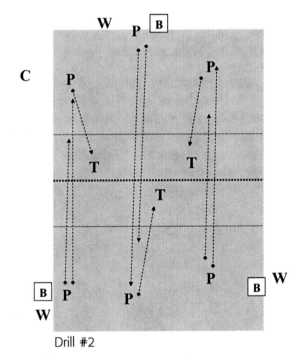

Drill #2

Drill #2: Passing Movement Warm-Up for Short and Deep Serves

Objective: To allow the players an opportunity to warm up with the proper footwork, while moving short and moving deep to pass serves, before receiving "live serves" from behind the end line

Set-up: Four players; a supply of volleyballs

Description: The players in each group of four should consist of a server, a passer, a target, and another player(s) waiting to serve who can hand the volleyballs to the active server. A player begins the drill by throwing or serving over the net from about 20 feet back from the net. She alternates serving short serves and deep serves to the passer in her group. The passer attempts to pass the served volleyball to the person in her group who is standing in the target area. The coach should position herself near one of the passers, so that she can provide feedback on the players' movement to the ball and passing technique. Each passer should be able to pass a certain number of balls to the target before that group rotates around, with everyone exchanging positions.

Coaching Point: Because passing a serve is a difficult skill, players need a chance to warm up, moving low and level to the ball coming over the net, before putting them in game-like situations with teammates serving, passing, setting, and hitting.

Variations: After all the players have rotated through their group, the servers can move back behind the end line to serve. Groups can also change places with other groups, passing from different areas on the court if sufficient time is available. If not, coaches should make sure the players vary their positions on the court the next time this drill is performed. The drill can also be changed by having the player serve the ball crosscourt or from different areas along the end line to the player in her group.

Drill #3: Passing Run-Throughs to the Net

Objective: To get the players warmed up by running up the sideline to pass a ball coming over the net to the target area

Set-up: All players; a supply of volleyballs; two ball baskets

Description: The players are divided into two groups, with each group having a basket of balls available. Player #1 starts near the net in the left-front position, with volleyballs from the basket being handed to her by player #2. The first player in the group starts in zone 1 (right back). She runs forward up the sideline to pass up the tossed ball from player #1 to the target area in the middle of their court. Player #3, who is positioned in that area to catch the ball, either returns it to the basket or bounces it under the net to player #2 to keep the drill going. After passing the ball, the players should return to the end of their same line. If the ball does not go to the target, the player should retrieve the ball and put it back in the basket. The same set-up is laid out on the other side of net with the other half of the players. The drill should continue for a certain number of good passes to the target.

Coaching Point: This drill should simulate players reading a tip and moving forward up the sideline to pass the ball up to the target area. The ball should be tossed low over the net (under the height of the antennae) and inside the attack area near the sideline. Players should stay low, while quickly moving up in the court to play the ball. They should angle their shoulders to the target area and stay on their feet throughout the drill. Make sure to switch in other players for P1 and P2 after so many passes.

Coaches should position themselves along the sideline to talk with the players after they make their pass.

Variations: After completing this drill, all the players should switch sides of their court so they are starting in left back (zone 5) and running up the sideline and passing to the target. The player tossing should move to the other side of the court as well, so she is also tossing short down the sideline. The toss can come from crosscourt for another variation

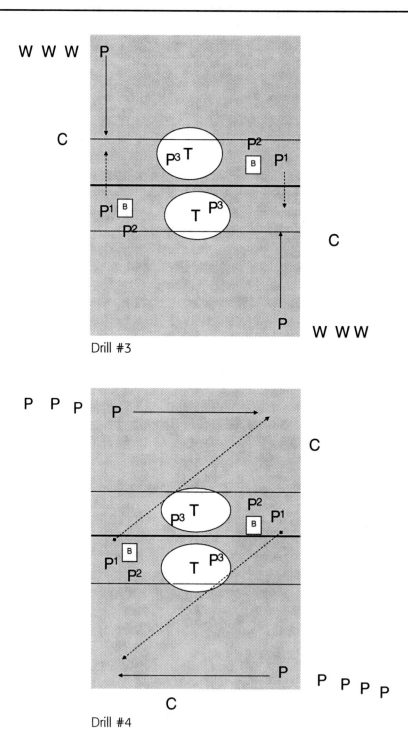

Drill #3

Drill #4

Drill #4: Passing Run-Throughs Along the End Line

Objective: To get the players warmed up by running along the end line to pass a ball coming over the net to the opposite corner

Set-up: All players; a supply of volleyballs; two ball baskets

Description: The players are divided into two groups, with each group having a basket of balls available. Player #1 starts on the other side of the net in the LF position (zone 4) with volleyballs from the basket being handed to her by player #2. The first player in the group starts in zone 1 or right back. She then runs along the end line toward zone 5 or left back to pass up a volleyball thrown from player #1. The pass should be directed back to the target area in the middle of their court. Player #3, who is positioned in that area to catch the ball, returns it to the basket or bounces it under the net to player #2 to keep the drill going. Players passing should return to the end of the same line. If the ball does not go to the target, the player should retrieve the ball and put it back in the basket. The same set-up is arranged on the other side of net with the other half of the players. The drill should continue for a certain number of good passes to the target.

Coaching Point: This drill should simulate players chasing a ball along the end line to pass the ball back over their shoulder to the target area. The ball should be over the net to the opposite deep corner near the sideline. Players should stay low, while quickly moving along the end line to play the ball. They should angle their shoulders back to the target area and stay on their feet throughout the drill. Coaches should make sure to switch in other players for P1 and P2 after so many passes. Coaches should position themselves behind the end line to talk with players after they make their pass and are returning to the end of the line.

Variations: After completing this drill, all the players should switch sides of their court so they are starting in left back (zone 5) and running toward zone 1 or right back along the end line. The player tossing should move to the other side of the court as well, so she is throwing the volleyball deep to the opposite corner.

Drill #5: Three-vs.-Three Short Court

Objective: To get the players warmed up for activity in a game-like fashion

Set-up: Six players; a supply of volleyballs; an extra antenna

Description: The players use half the court inside the attack area. Six more players could be using the other half of the court, which can be divided by the antenna in the middle of the net. The players simply put the ball in motion over the net with an overhead set from behind the attack line, and the other team has three contacts using an overhead set before sending the ball back over the net. Players should rotate serving as their team wins the rally. They should play rally scoring to 10 and then switch the teams around until they have all played each other.

Coaching Point: This drill is an excellent way to have the players warm up and get lots of contacts with the volleyball over the net. Players learn better ball control and body control around the net. This activity is also a fun, competitive game for the players. The coach should be moving along the sideline near the attack area so that the players can be observed on both sides of the net.

Variations: Players should quickly move to a serve, pass, set, hit game as soon as possible by adding a blocker against the hitter. This drill can also be played as doubles in the short court.

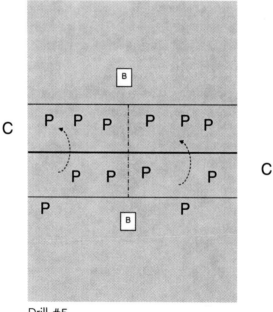

Drill #5

Drill #6: Communication

Objective: To teach the players the types of situations in a game and words to be used to describe each situation while the ball is in play

Set-up: A chalkboard or whiteboard; chalk or pen; all players

Description: The coach and team discuss the types of situations that happen during a game and the word or phrase that the entire team should be calling out to describe it. A designated player should write each of the aforementioned situations and its verbal signal on the board, while the team talks about it. Examples of such a situation include when an attacker tips the ball, the setter dumps the ball, an attacker is hitting down the line, or hitting an off-speed shot, etc. The team and the coach should discuss what types of drills can help them learn to call out these important words as soon as they see a particular situation in a game.

Coaching Point: It is important that the team takes leadership in determining the appropriate words or phrases for identifying a situation and how the players can learn to improve communicating these to their teammates during a game.

Variations: Drills can be set up with teams only scoring points when they are communicating the words they determined to be important.

Drill #7: Physical-Training Circuit

Objective: To provide the players with a variety of physical-training activities that can help them improve their effectiveness on the court

Set-up: All players; surgical tubing; a medicine ball; jump ropes; a stopwatch

Description: The players are divided into six groups, with each one going to a different station. The activity at each station should last 15 seconds. The entire group should then run six laps around the entire volleyball court, at which point the groups then rotate stations. After another 15 seconds of activity, the team runs five laps in the opposite direction around the court and rotates stations. This scenario continues until the players are only running one lap around the court. The different stations can be set up using the following activities: surgical tubing tied around the volleyball standard for each player in the group (e.g., players pull the tubing using an overhead serving motion or a spiking motion); forward or lateral lunges in place; crunches; an overhead medicine ball throw or chest pass; regular push-ups, or performed with the hands close together or with the feet elevated; back hyperextensions on the floor; tuck jumps; step-ups on a bleacher; dips on a bleacher; split squat jumps; butt-kicks or high knee lifts in place; jump rope; squats; etc.

Coaching Point: The circuit consists of six stations, with a variety of the aforementioned activities. The activity between sets can vary as well, with bounding, sprints, or jumping rope. There should be 45 seconds of rest before beginning the next station. The entire circuit of six "15-second" stations should take approximately 18 minutes. If the stations last 20 seconds, the circuit will take 24 minutes.

Variations: This type of circuit could be performed at the beginning of practice, the middle of practice, or the end of practice. It should only be done a few times a week, in order to allow the players time to physically recover completely.

2

Ball-Control Drills

Drill #8: Two-vs.-Two Narrow Court Tipping

Objective: To help the players learn how to control the ball on a narrow court, read the attacker, and play up a tipped ball, as well as moving forward and backward quickly

Set-up: Four players; a supply of volleyballs; a scoreboard

Description: The players are divided up into partners. An extra set of antennae are put on the inside areas of the narrow court to help designate the inside lines. Portable scoreboards are used for each court if more than one group is doing this drill. One player serves, while the other partner is at the net ready to block and set. The serve is passed, and the partner sets it to her teammate who passed the ball, so that she can make an approach and tip the ball. The hitter must tip the ball over the net around the blocker. The defender should get into position to read the attacker and see the ball around the blocker's hands. Players switch positions after they play the ball over the net. The deep player comes up, and after attacking the ball, stays at the net. The player who set the ball at the net backpedals quickly to the end line and comes back in to play defense. The drill can be scored, with teams playing rally scoring to five points. Other teams then rotate on the court to play.

Coaching Point: This drill helps players learn to control their serve by having a narrow court. The pass has to be somewhat controlled for the other player to get to it and make a set. This drill is a good exercise to get the players moving forward and backward and practice controlling the ball in a smaller court.

Variations: Teams can rotate around playing a round-robin format until they have all played each other. Games can be played to more than five points.

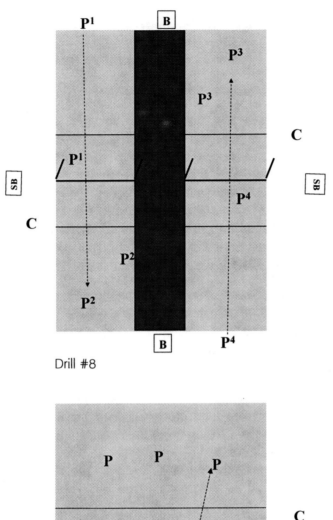

Drill #8

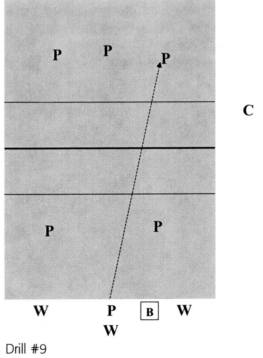

Drill #9

Drill #9: Triples with Individual Scoring

Objective: To have the players work hard as individuals to score the most points

Set-up: All players; a supply of volleyballs; a scoreboard

Description: This drill involves a regular game of triples or Queen of the court. The individuals on the far side of the court only get a point when they win a rally. When they lose the rally, they should retrieve the volleyball, and each player should go to the end of the next line. For example, if the players were in the middle, they should rotate to the line on the left side of the court. The player in the front of the right sideline should then serve and enter the court to play out the rally, with the front person from each of the other two lines on the court with them. If the serving team wins the rally, the players on that team run to the other side of the court or the winner's side of the court and get ready to receive a serve.

Coaching Point: The coach should designate someone to keep the individual player's scores. Each player will only score a point when she wins a rally while on the far side of the net. The players should be rotating lines and coming out on the court with different players each time. This requirement helps show which players are able to win the most with different teammates.

Variations: Triples can also be played keeping the same teammates and keeping score by teams. Coaches could also increase camaraderie by having the players stay in teams by positions, such as the setters on one team, middles on another team, defensive players on another team, and outside hitters on another team. This drill could also be performed with players only hitting from behind the attack line to improve back-row attacking.

Drill #10: 1-vs.-1, 2-vs.-2, 3-vs.-3, 4-vs.-4, 5-vs.-5

Objective: To provides players with the opportunity to play with all of their teammates and improve their individual skills and ball control

Set-up: All players; a supply of volleyballs; an extra antenna; a white board and marker

Description: The drill involves the players playing a round-robin tournament schedule. Each player plays every other player in a 1-vs.-1 game, with rally scoring to seven points. One player serves to the other player, who then passes the serve up to herself, sets the ball to herself, and then attacks the ball into the narrow court. The other player then digs it up, sets it, and attacks it back into the court. Two games should be going on at a time on each court. The results should be recorded on a white board, and then the next games should start as soon as two players finish their game. After everyone has played one another, the players are divided into doubles teams and then play a round-robin format of games to seven points on the narrow court. In this part of the drill, one player serves to a player on the other team who then passes the ball to her teammate, who will then set it back to her teammate to attack it. The team on defense should have one player at the net as a blocker and the other teammate back playing defense around the blocker. This tournament continues until all of the players have completed the round robin. The players are then divided into groups of three and play the round-robin tournament on a full court. This arrangement continues until they finish the 5-vs.-5 round-robin tournament, playing to seven points rally scoring on a full court.

Coaching Point: Coaches should keep track of the total wins of each player in each phase of the drill.

Variations: It may take several practice sessions to complete all aspects of the competition.

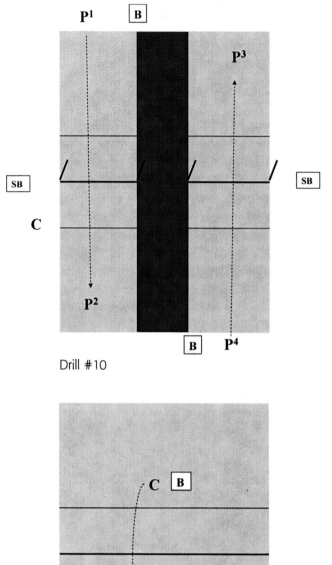

Drill #10

Drill #11

Drill #11: Figure It Out

Objective: To train the players to find the ball and problem solve while the ball is in the air

Set-up: Three players; a supply of volleyballs

Description: The drill involves three-person groups. The three players start the drill lying on their stomachs on the end line facing away from the net. The coach blows the whistle and puts the ball over the net into their court. The players must quickly get up and find the ball. One player has to pass it up, the second player has to set it, and the third player has to jump and spike the ball over the net into the other court to earn one point. They then retrieve their ball, and the next group of three gets into position on the endline. This drill keeps going until the team has scored 15 points or each group of three has scored twice.

Coaching Point: All factors considered, the degree of difficulty of this drill is based on where the coach sends the ball into the court. The ball may come over the net near one sideline, close to the net, in the middle of the court, or at the endline. This drill helps players learn to deal with broken plays or playing out-of-system with a poor first pass or dig in a game. It also teaches them to try to set themselves up for an attack, instead of giving the opponents a free ball.

Variations: This drill could be done with two or four players. The players could also start in a different formation at the endline or could be positioned standing at the net facing the endline when the ball comes over. A player could be used to send the ball over the net trying to make it tough on their teammates to play the ball.

Drill #12: Follow the Leader

Objective: To have the players have numerous contacts with the volleyball, while under pressure to keep the ball in play

Set-up: Six players; one volleyball

Description: The drill involves designating one player as the "leader" of the court who starts on one sideline of the court, positioning the rest of the group near the other sideline. The front person in the group sets the ball to the single player (the "leader") and then goes to the end of the line. The single player sets the ball back to the next person, and that player sets the ball and goes to the end of the line. This scenario continues until each player by herself has set the ball 10 times. Without stopping the drill, the next person sets the ball to the single person and then follows the set to take her place as the "leader." This rotation continues without stopping until every person has been the single player and has set the ball 10 times.

Coaching Point: This drill is a good exercise to get lots of contacts, while communicating and moving around the court. Players should count out loud so they can keep up with when they will need to switch leaders. Each player should be calling the ball before she plays it. She should also call out the name of the player to whom she is directing the ball to for the next contact.

Variations: This drill can be done using underhand or forearm passing. It can also be done across the net.

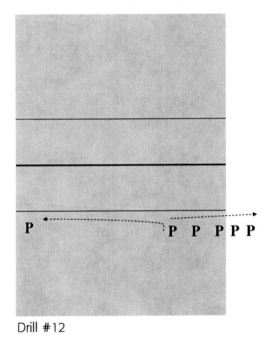

Drill #12

Drill #13: Set and Move

Objective: To help players learn to concentrate each time they contact the ball under pressure

Set-up: Two players; one volleyball

Description: The drill involves dividing the players into groups of two. The players begin on opposite sidelines from one another. The first player sets the ball to her partner and then runs around her partner and back to her own sideline, while her partner sets the ball high to herself, before setting it back to the sideline. That player then takes off to run around her partner, while her partner sets the ball high to herself and then back to the other sideline. This drill continues until each player has run around her partner 10 times.

Coaching Point: This drill is a good conditioning activity that helps improve quickness to the ball during a rally.

Variations: The partner may need to set the ball twice to herself in order to give the player enough time to sprint across the court and then back to their sideline before the ball gets back to her. This can also be done across the net with the players on each attack line.

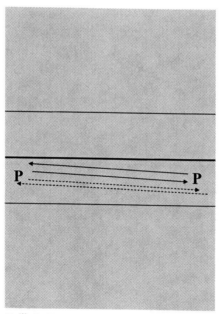

Drill #13

Drill #14: Front Set, Back Set, Crosscourt Set

Objective: To train all players to set different types of sets when needed

Set-up: Three players; one volleyball

Description: One player starts on a sideline, another player starts in the middle of the court, and the third player starts on the opposite sideline. The first player frontsets to the player in the middle, who then backsets to the player behind her on the other sideline. That player then frontsets the ball completely crosscourt to the first player. This pattern continues 10 times. The players switch positions until they have been in all three positions setting a frontset halfway across the court, a backset halfway across the court, and a frontset the full width of the court.

Coaching Point: It is important for all the players to have the skill necessary to set the ball various distances in front of them and behind them. This drill also helps players learn that they need to have their shoulders square to the direction where they want their backset to go.

Variations: The drill could be set up so the players must be able to do these sets 10 times in a row without making a setting error. Add a fourth player off the net to add angles.

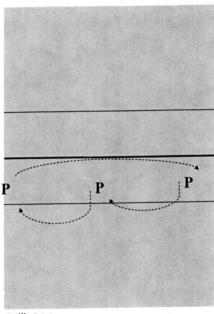

Drill #14

Drill #15: Metronome

Objective: To train the players to learn the desired tempo for their passes so that all of the players will pass a ball the same height

Set-up: All players; a supply of volleyballs

Description: The drill involves dividing the team into two-person groups. The partners are positioned around the court on both sides of the net. One partner will be on the attack line and the other partner will be near the end line. One player on the court is designated as the "leader," who tells the rest of the players when to toss their ball. The "leader" also counts out loud for the team each time they touch the ball. The players on the attack line then toss a ball to their partner. That player then attempts to pass the ball antenna height (10-feet high) back to their partner. All of the balls continue to stay in play with the passes going back and forth antenna height. The purpose of the drill is to have all the players at the attack line contacting the ball at the same time and then all the players near the end line at the same time. The drill ends when the team can achieve that scenario for 10 repetitions.

Coaching Point: This drill may take a little while for all of the players to find the correct rhythm with the "leader." The "leader" should be in the middle of the court, so that the players on that side of the net can see where that ball is and try to keep the same timing going back and forth. The "leader" may need to have a different colored ball to distinguish her ball from the other volleyballs.

Variations: This drill can be done with an overhead setting simulating balls being received as a free ball that is being set the same height.

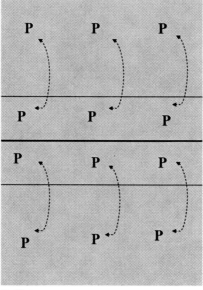

Drill #15

Drill #16: One-Minute Ball-Control Drills

Objective: To help players learn to concentrate under pressure each time they contact the ball

Set-up: All players; one volleyball for every two players

Description: The activity involves dividing the players into two-person groups. The partners are positioned opposite each other near each sideline. The exercise involves performing a series of various ball-control drills. Each one of the drills should be done without any errors or illegal contacts for one minute. If one player makes a mistake, the entire team starts the minute over. A player sets the ball to her partner, who sets to herself and then sets the ball back to her partner. This exercise could also be done with the player setting to herself, turning 180 degrees, and backsetting to her partner across the court.

Coaching Point: A couple of these drills could be done near the beginning of practice to allow the players to get a number of successful contacts before they engage in group drills.

Variations: These types of drills can be used to practice underhand or forearm passing. The players could pass the ball up to themselves and back to their partner or pass it up and turn 180 degrees and pass back to their partner. They could also just turn 90 degrees and laterally pass it back to their partner, alternating the direction they turn each time—e.g., first to the right, and then to the left.

Drill #17: Three-vs.-Three Narrow Court

Objective: To help players learn to have more control when they serve or spike a ball

Set-up: Six players; a supply of volleyballs; an extra antenna; floor tape

Description: The drill requires placing the antenna on the net in the middle of the court. Floor tape can be used to mark a line to make it a narrow court. This drill involves a 3-vs.-3 game on a long narrow court. The drill begins by having one player on a team serve to the team on the other side of the net. The players on the receiving team pass, set, and hit the ball into the opponent's court trying to score. The rally continues until one team scores a point. The game could be played until one team scores five points. The teams then rotate around, with each team playing against one another.

Coaching Point: This drill is a good exercise to have one player blocking and two players digging behind her. The drill is designed to demonstrate how part of the court will be cut off by the block and how important it is to play defense around the blocker. Tipping is allowed by the attacker.

Variations: This drill can also be done with the teams competing on diagonal courts.

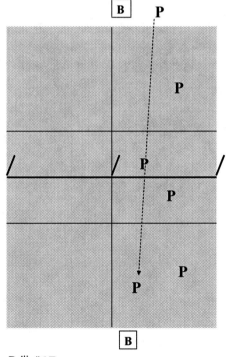

Drill #17

Drill #18: Reaction Time

Objective: To improve the reaction time of players when covering their hitter

Set-up: Two players; a supply of volleyballs; a flat surface or wall; tape or chalk

Description: A piece of tape or chalkline is placed on the wall at the height of the top of the net. The players are divided into two-person groups. One player faces the wall just a few feet away. Her partner has a ball which she tosses or throws so that it hits the wall above the tape and drops down close to her partner. That player tries to dig the ball up away from the wall (net) to her teammate behind her. The partner should vary her tosses so it comes from the right and the left, as well as both harder and softer, so the distance it bounces off the wall varies. The player at the wall should be able to dig up 10 balls successfully, so her teammate could play the ball. As the players get better, they can be given a target zone closer to the wall (net) where the setter may be located for a quicker transition.

Coaching Point: This drill demonstrates to the players the importance of being low, with their arms outstretched, and being ready to react to a ball being blocked down into their court. The players should focus on the wall at the tape, just like they would focus on the blocker's hands during a game.

Variations: This drill could also involve three players, who could be positioned in a semi-circle at the wall, just as they would be around a live attacker. This arrangement would provide another challenge—deciding who will take the ball landing in between them.

Drill #19: Sending Free Balls to Targets

Objective: To train the players to give their opponents a difficult free ball to pass

Set-up: One player; a supply of volleyballs; floor tape or chalk

Description: The drill involves one player who is positioned out on the court. The coach tosses a ball up to the player, who then must "free ball" the ball over the net to certain target zones that are marked on the opposite court.

Coaching Point: The areas of the court the players should be aiming for are zone one or deep in the right back of the court where the setter may be vacating to get to the front row to set the ball. Two other possible target areas are within two feet of the endline or either sideline. It is important to emphasize that the player should have her shoulders square to the target she is trying to hit. The time needed to perform this drill is well spent because it decreases the likelihood that the opponents will receive an easy free ball.

Variations: Coaches can leave the targets or zones marked on the court during a six-on-six scrimmage and reward the team with a bonus point if the players send a free ball into one of these areas during play. This stipulation will increase their focus on the concept of not giving opponents easy free balls during actual matches.

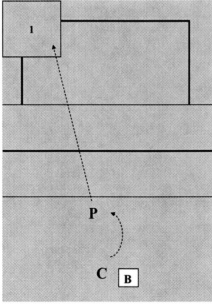

Drill #19

3

Serve and Serve-Receive Drills

Drill #20: Aggressive Serving for Accuracy

Objective: To teach the players to serve aggressively within reason

Set-up: All players; two baskets of volleyballs

Description: Players are positioned at the endline in their serving positions. One person should be responsible for recording the serves and errors for each player. Each player is required to serve 10 "aggressive" serves into the court. "Aggressive serves" land near a sideline or endline or cross the net under the top of the antenna (i.e., three feet above the top of the net). If the serve is not aggressive, it does not count as one of the 10 serves, but there is no penalty. If the player makes a mistake serving (e.g., into the net or out of bounds), she receives an error. Each player is allowed two errors while attempting to hit 10 aggressive serves. Once a player makes a third error, a good serve is deducted from her total. As such, for every error after two, the player loses credit for one of her good serves. For example, hitting eight good serves with a third error makes it seven good serves. Another missed serve makes it six good serves, and so on, until the player has hit 10 aggressive serves. The rest of the players are passing and rotate over as servers.

Coaching Point: This drill is designed to emphasize the point that players should serve aggressively with control.

Variations: Coaches may want to start with fewer than 10 aggressive serves and perhaps allow more penalty-free errors, while working up to 10 serves with two allowable errors before good serves are subtracted.

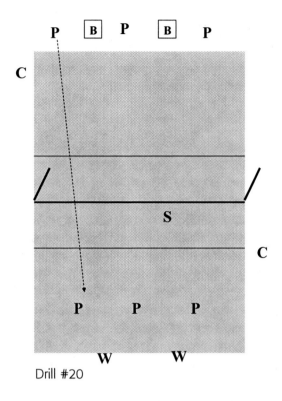

Drill #20

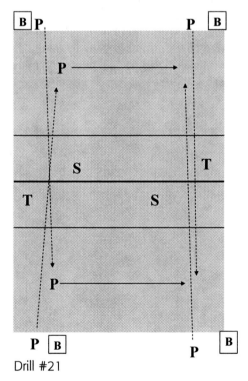

Drill #21

Drill #21: One-Minute Passing

Objective: To train the player receiving the serve to stay low and move in a level position back and forth quickly across the court

Set-up: All players; four baskets of volleyballs; a stopwatch

Description: The drill involves having a player ready to serve outside each corner of the court, with a supply of volleyballs for each of them. Another player is on each side of the court who will be receiving the serves. There is also a setter in the target area on each side of the net who is counting the number of perfect passes to the target for their passer. The setter can set to a target area for an outside set. The drill starts with the timer blowing a whistle. The server down the line then serves the ball to the passer down the line. The passer attempts to pass the ball and then quickly shuffles in a low position toward the other sideline. The next server then serves the ball down that line to the passer, who passes the ball and shuffles back to the other sideline. The servers should be ready to serve the ball as soon as the player has passed the serve. The drill lasts for approximately one minute until the whistle is blown. The player with the fewest number of passes during that minute is subsequently to perform a predetermined number of calisthenics, such as 10 push-ups, 10 sit-ups, or 10 lunges, etc. The players change positions so there are new passers and new servers, etc. The drill continues until each player has been through as a passer four times.

Coaching Point: The drill is designed to enable the passer to learn to concentrate to pass the ball to the target first before beginning to move to the other side of the court. This drill is a good exercise for building leg strength and efficient footwork. Coaches should keep statistics on as many passing drills as possible to determine the best passers on the team.

Variations: The servers can serve crosscourt to the passer instead of down the line.

Drill #22: Servers vs. Passers

Objective: To practice making and receiving tough serves

Set-up: All players; a supply of volleyballs for each court

Description: The players are divided into two groups, with half on each side of the court. Three players are passing on each side of the court, with the other players behind the endline waiting for their turn to serve. Two people are assigned to keep track of the number of perfect passes and missed serves for each team. Both sides of the court are doing this drill at the same time, but they are competing against one another. One player serves the ball over the net to the passers. The ball is passed up to the target area. If it is a perfect pass, that team gets a "3" recorded. If a server makes a serving error, her team will have one of their perfect passes or "3's" deleted. Each group of passers receives 10 serves, with an extra player taking the place of whoever just passed the ball. After 10 receptions for each side of the court, the players switch around with new servers and new passers. At the end of the drill, each group should have had 50 serves and/or 50 passes. The group with the fewest number of perfect passes is given a pre-set number of calisthenics to perform, such as one minute of push-ups or sits-ups.

Coaching Point: It is important that the two people recording perfect passes and missed serves are sitting close together and telling each other if there was a missed serve, etc. The servers need to take a little time between serves to make sure the results of the pass are recorded.

Variations: Setters can be used on the court to set each pass to a specific target or person who is positioned as a left-side or right-side hitter.

Drill #23: Passing Circuit

Objective: To increase the number of repetitions the players get at the beginning of practice for forearm-ball control, free balls, down balls, and receiving serves

Set-up: All players; a supply of volleyballs; two courts set up

Description: This drill involves performing a circuit that can be done for 7-10 minutes at each station of the circuit. The players are divided into groups of three and sent to different areas in the gym. One group can work outside the courts, while the other two groups each need their own court. One group has each player passing the volleyball in the air to herself, while trying to get to 50 in a row and staying in a controlled area off the court. Another option is to have each player pass the ball against the wall into a small area above net height 50 times in a row. The second group is working with a coach or another player who is sending free balls over the net. They are passing the balls to the target area. The players in that group will also be receiving down balls coming across the net and passing them to the target area. The third group is on another court receiving serves from over the net and passing them to the target area.

Coaching Point: This circuit provides players with a large number of repetitions to work on forearm ball control in a variety of ways. For example, either coaches can send the balls over the net or players can do so, while coaches instruct.

Variations: The setters can work with the free-ball/down-ball group and the serve-receive group in order to get extra repetitions of setting balls to a target person or area at the net.

Drill #24: Serve and Catch in Zones

Objective: To help players learn the different zones of the court when serving

Set-up: All players with partners; a supply of volleyballs

Description: The drill involves dividing the players into two-person groups. One player stands in her serving position along the endline with a volleyball. Her partner is standing next to her. The player without the ball takes off running around the outside of the court and the net support or standard, while simultaneously the server calls out the zone into which she is going to serve (1 through 6). The player who is running must get into that zone and catch the serve for it to count as a successful attempt. The partners then switch to the opposite side of the court, and the other partner serves to a zone, while her partner sprints to get into position to catch the serve. The drill continues until each player has 10 catches.

Coaching Point: This drill is also a good physical-conditioning activity, given that the players are sprinting to the zone called out. This drill can be designed to be competitive by declaring the first set of partners to finish serving and catching to all six zones as the winner of the drill.

Variations: This drill could have the player sprint over to the correct zone and then actually pass the serve to the target to be successful.

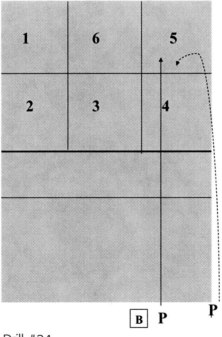

Drill #24

Drill #25: Partner Seam Passing

Objective: To help teammates understand seam responsibilities when receiving a served volleyball

Set-up: Four players; a supply of volleyballs

Description: Two players begin the drill in their passing positions on the court next to one another, which could be the left and middle or the middle and right if the team uses a three-person reception pattern. A server is located across the net. Prior to the serve, the passers should determine which one of them will pass a ball served short in the seam (in front) and which one will pass a ball served deep in the seam (behind). The partners receive serves until they achieve a certain number of good passes to the target. The groups should rotate so that all players get to work on covering the seams in the team passing-reception pattern.

Coaching Point: The passer closest to the server should take the short seam, and the one furthest away should cover the deep seam. The players should hold out their arms to show their teammate what area they plan to cover. Coaches should have players serve from different areas along the endline to make sure the partners adjust their seam responsibilities, based on where the server is in relationship to them.

Variations: The team should be able to use different passing patterns with two, three, or four players, with each one having a different number of seams that she needs to be ready to cover.

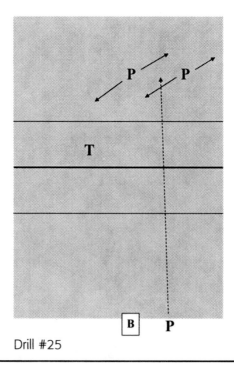

Drill #25

Drill #26: Game Warm-Up Serving and Passing

Objective: To make sure the players get as many opportunities serving and passing the volleyball from different areas in a short amount of time

Set-up: All players; a supply of volleyballs; a stopwatch

Description: The players are divided into three groups based on their positions (outsides, middles, and defensive players). Each group will serve and pass within their own group for a certain amount of time or repetitions. When the time is up or the repetitions undertaken, each group then moves to another area of the court and repeats the drill for a certain amount of time or repetitions.

Coaching Point: The allotted time in each position may be two-to-five minutes before moving to a different area of the court. The repetitions may be five-to-ten serves or passes before rotating. This drill keeps everyone involved, with their focus on a certain area of the court. Each group moves until the members of the group have passed from the left, middle, and right side of the court. The middles work on serving and passing short serves to their group, just like they would need to pass in a game.

Variations: The groups can be set up with a different position player in each group (a setter/defensive player, middle, and outside).

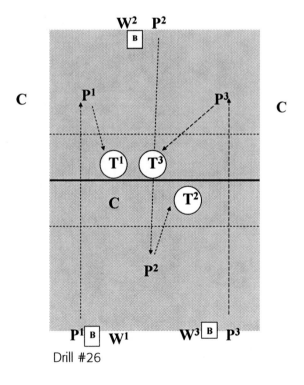

Drill #26

Drill #27: Short and Deep Serves

Objective: To help the players learn to serve to and pass from different zones of the court

Set-up: All players; a supply of volleyballs

Description: Each player is assigned a partner. Across the net, a player's partner stands in an area of the court to receive the serve. If she stands in one of the zones along the net (2, 3, or 4), her partner serves a ball to her in that area, and she then passes the ball to the setting target at the net. On the next repetition, the partner should pick one of the deep zones in the back of the court (5, 6, or 1). This drill continues with the players alternating short and deep until they have served 10 balls in the correct zones.

Coaching Point: It is important that the players make all the serves look alike before they serve so that the opponent does not know whether the ball will be served short or deep.

Variations: Any time the team is in a six-on-six scrimmage, the players must alternate short and deep serves each time the ball is served. This stipulation forces all players to get practice in game-like situations involving having to serve short or deep.

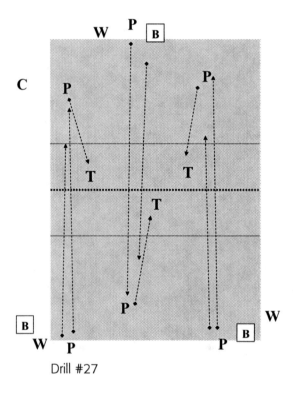

Drill #27

4

Setting Drills

Drill #28: Setter-Footwork Training

Objective: To teach the setter how to move efficiently to all areas of the court from the target area to set the ball

Set-up: Setters; a supply of volleyballs; floor tape

Description: Initially, this drill is conducted without using volleyballs. The setter starts in the target area, takes a step off the net, and gets square to her target (left front hitter) marked with floor tape. She then transitions quickly back to the net, takes a step off the net in a different direction, and gets square to her target (left-front hitter), before transitioning back to the net. This continues until the setter has done this sequence behind, to the side, and in front several times. The setter then repeats these series, taking two steps off the net, etc. Next, the setter repeats the series again, taking three steps off the net, squaring up to the left-front position, and transitioning back to the net. Once the setter has been through all of these options and has moved quickly with the correct footwork, the drill begins again by tossing a ball so that the setter must move off the net one step and set the ball to the target area or left-front position. This series is continued so that the setter gets a predetermined number of repetitions of setting the ball from off the net.

Coaching Point: This drill provides a good opportunity to work with the setter without the distraction of a volleyball or other players involved. The players can perform this drill on their own so that they are warmed up and ready to go when a live ball is put in play, and they have to move to set it.

Variations: Instead of having the ball tossed to the setter, the ball can be passed from a player so that the setter can read the passer's arms and get ready to move to the correct position to pass the ball. The focus should remain on the setter, using the correct footwork to get into the best position to set the ball to the attacker.

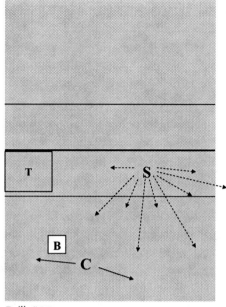

Drill #28

Drill #29: Wall Setting

Objective: To help players learn how to use their wrists when setting or overhead passing the volleyball

Set-up: All players; one volleyball per player

Description: The drill involves having each player stand about one foot from a wall with a flat surface. To initiate the drill, the player puts the volleyball and her hands up over her forehead and begins setting the ball to the wall. She continues this fast set for a certain amount of time, building up to one minute without stopping.

Coaching Point: This activity is designed to increase the use of the wrist in setting. The arms should be bent at the elbow and relatively still, with only the wrists moving to keep the ball going against the wall.

Variations: The players should perform this drill with their dominant hand and then with their non-dominant hand. This drill can help setters needing to building up their strength in their wrists for setting the ball across the court or dumping the ball more powerfully.

Drill #30: Setting Tight Passes

Objective: To teach the setter how to move closely around the net to set a tight pass or dig

Set-up: Setters; a supply of volleyballs

Description: The drill can involve either having the setter start at the net ready to play the ball or performing the activity next to a flat wall. The setter should be taught the correct movement of how to set the ball close to the net by keeping the right forearm parallel (or straight up and down) to the net. The left arm can still involve having the elbow away from the body. Initially, the drill starts by having a ball tossed close to the net from a short distance. The setter should use this prescribed arm position to contact the ball with her hands and push it outside to the left-side attacker. In addition, the setter should be required to work on setting quick attacks to the middle with a tight pass, using just the right hand to quickly tap the ball up in the air for the attacker.

Coaching Point: Players should be required to work on the proper hand and arm position for setting before a ball is tossed to allow them to learn how to move their arms in the appropriate position without touching the net.

Variations: The setter could work on jump setting and using one hand to set the ball. The drill could also have live passers work on passing tight sets.

Drill #31: Setting From Around the Court

Objective: To teach the setter how to chase down a ball outside the target area and set the left-side hitter from all different areas of the court

Set-up: Setters; a supply of volleyballs; floor tape

Description: The setters start the drill at the net. The coach or another player is on the court tossing volleyballs to different zones of the court marked with floor tape. This drill is designed to give the setter repetitions in setting the ball from all areas of the court. Initially, the setter begins the drill at the net in the setting position. The coach then tosses a ball to zone 1. The setter must quickly come off the net to get into the correct position under the ball, get square to the target (left front), and set the ball to a player or target in that area. This pattern continues with the setter moving to each of the six zones and setting a high outside ball to left front from zone 1. She then moves back to the net, then to zone 3, zone, 4, zone 5 and zone 6. This drill can be conducted much like a game of horse in basketball, where the players are only allowed to continue in the drill when they make a successful set from that zone.

Coaching Point: This drill offers a good opportunity to work with the setters on the proper footwork and efficiency in getting off the net to the ball.

Variations: The drill can involve two setters competing with each other and possibly a right-side player. The setter may also go through the rotations, setting the ball with a forearm pass.

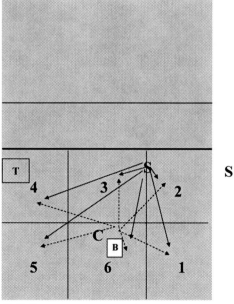

Drill #31

Drill #32: Setter Dumps to Targets

Objective: To help the setter practice scoring on the second contact at different areas on the court

Set-up: Setters; floor tape or chalk; a supply of volleyballs

Description: The drill involves working off different target areas of the court into which the setter needs to be able to dump the ball. The ball is tossed to the setter to start the drill. She then jump sets the ball and either sets the ball toward an outside hitter or dumps the ball to one of the pre-designated target areas. The drill can be set up like playing "horse" in basketball. The setter has to dump the ball in each one of these areas to complete the drill. The ball should be given to the setter from all areas of the court.

Coaching Point: The setter needs to be accurate when jump setting the ball to the outside hitters so that she can contact the ball high enough above the net to try to score aggressively on the dump.

Variations: The setter can be required to dump the ball against a full team, giving the setter different points for scoring in certain spots.

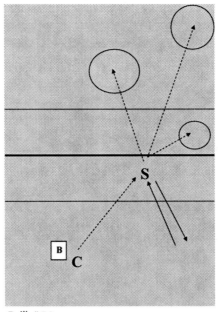

Drill #32

Drill #33: Sets to Targets

Objective: To help the setter(s) get some extra opportunities to work on setting accuracy

Set-up: Three players; a supply of volleyballs; chalk or floor tape for targets

Description: The drill begins by having a player serve or free ball the volleyball over the net to a passer. The setter then transitions to her position at the net and then sets the volleyball to certain targets around the court. The target zones may be marked on the floor with chalk or appropriate tape.

Coaching Point: The target zones should be just far enough off the net so that an attacker can take a full swing at the ball without touching the net on her follow through. Too many times, the volleyball is set too close to the net, and the hitter cannot take a full swing. The target being off the net also provides the attacker with a better opportunity to hit around the block. Coaches should make sure to include numerous target zones along the net, as well as for the back-row attacks.

Variations: If other players are available, they can be the targets for the setter by standing on the ground facing the net with their hitting arm up in the air as the target. This step will give the setter realistic feedback on whether she had a good set or not. They can also pass and then hit the set.

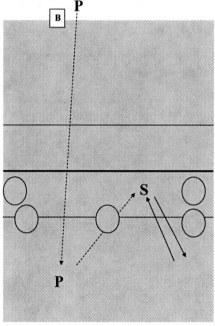

Drill #33

Drill #34: Three-Player Movement Setting

Objective: To have a player get multiple contacts with the volleyball to improve her ball-control skills

Set-up: Three players; one volleyball

Description: The drill involves having to of the players start on one sideline with the ball, while the third player is positioned on the other sideline. The player with the ball overhead sets the ball to the player across the court and follows the set. Each player sets the ball and follows her set for one minute or a certain number of good contacts. If the ball is dropped or set illegally, either the entire team starts over at zero or the minute starts over.

Coaching Point: The coach can determine the height of the set to increase the difficulty of the drill.

Variations: This drill can be done with underhand or forearm passing. It can also be done over the net.

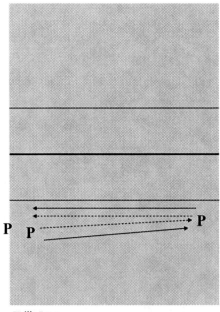

Drill #34

Drill #35: Right Sides and Liberos Setting

Objective: To develop the ability to set an accurate, hittable ball to the attacker if the setter has to dig or pass on the first contact

Set-up: Right sides and liberos; a supply of volleyballs; floor tape or chalk

Description: The drill begins with the right side jumping to block. As they land, the coach tosses a volleyball toward the net for the right side to set. They then block, land, and turn around to find the ball coming up, which they then set to the left side of the court to a predetermined target. The target can be an area marked on the floor with tape or chalk. The coach then tosses a ball, which requires the libero to run in from the back row (middle or left back) and set, using an underhand pass to the right side to attack.

Coaching Point: The right side or opposite player and the libero could participate in every setting drill with the setters. The libero should set the ball with an underhand pass, as allowed by the rules. The more accurate the right side becomes at setting a "hittable" ball to the left side attacker, the more likely it will be for them to learn to set a quick set to the middle hitters.

Variations: When having the setter work on digging a ball to the target area, the right side and libero could be working on setting the second ball to various attackers in different areas of the court. A passer can be added in the right back to pass the ball up to the right side to set and then pass up to the libero to come in and underhand set to the right side to attack the ball. A left-side attacker can be added to the drill to hit the balls being set.

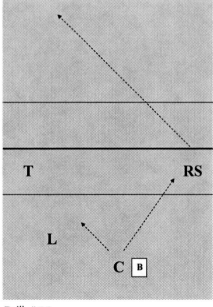

Drill #35

Drill #36: Lateral Sets

Objective: To learn how to legally make a lateral set of the volleyball along the net

Set-up: All players; one volleyball per two players

Description: The drill involves dividing the team into two-person groups. One player is on a line, while her partner is 20 feet away on the same line. The person with the ball tosses it up to herself, sets it straight up, then makes a quarter-turn to the right, and sets the ball laterally to her partner along the line. The partner then sets the ball to herself, makes a quarter-turn to the right, and sets the ball laterally to her partner along the line. This pattern continues, with the players turning the opposite direction each time (first turn to the right, next time to the left, next time to the right, etc.)

Coaching Point: It is important the players learn how to make a legal lateral set if the volleyball is too tight to the net and they need to set the ball without touching the net. Making a proper legal set requires the ball to leave both hands at the same time without a double contact.

Variations: The players could try this drill near a wall or next to the net for a certain number of repetitions without touching anything.

Drill #37: Changing Directions

Objective: To train the setter to set the ball away from the flow of the game

Set-up: Six players; a supply of volleyballs

Description: One player is a server behind the endline. On the other side of the net, two players are passers, while another player is in the setting position or coming out of the back row from behind a passer when the ball is served. The other two players serve as targets in the right front and left front. The ball is served and passed to the setter. The setter then sets in the opposite direction from the direction she has moved to set the ball. If the setter has moved from the target zone toward the left side of the court, she should back set to the right side of the court target. If she moves backward toward the right side of the court, she should set outside to the left-front target. The drill continues until a certain number of sets land in the assigned target areas.

Coaching Point: While the setter should always strive to be in a neutral position when setting, it is important for her to learn to set away from the flow created by the pass. If the pass is a good one and the setter doesn't need to move, she can set any of the attack zones, including the back row. This drill could also be used to help the setter to learn to create a certain flow with the attack pattern and to set away from that flow to create an opportunity for her team's attacker to score against one blocker.

Variations: Live attackers could be added to the drill for the setter to set, as well as add blockers on the other side of the net trying to read the setter.

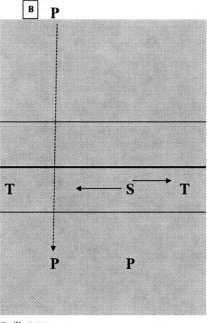

Drill #37

Drill #38: Decision Sets

Objective: To train the setter to see the position of the opposing blockers

Set-up: Eight players; a supply of volleyballs

Description: The drill starts with a player serving the ball over the net to three players on the court as passers. One of the passers then pass the ball to the setter, who can either start in the front row or come out of the back row. The drill involves three blockers who are waiting to block the attacker. The middle blocker should take a step to the right or left before the setter sets the passed ball. The setter then notices the movement and sets the opposite direction that the middle blocker stepped. The attackers then attack the set ball, trying to score versus their blocker. The drill continues until the setter has successfully set the ball in the opposite direction a certain number of times.

Coaching Point: The setter should be able to make an "eye check" toward the outside antenna, allowing her to see out of her peripheral vision any movement of the blockers on the other side of the net, as well as seeing the attackers available on the court. She achieves this objective by keeping her head still, while taking her eyes off the passed ball momentarily before the ball gets to her to glance toward the antenna.

Variations: This drill can be done with a coach or player acting as the middle blocker during setting repetitions performed without the rest of the team. Bonus points could be given to the setter for successfully setting the ball in the opposite direction.

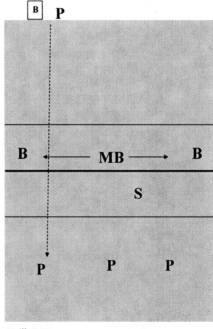

Drill #38

5

Attacking Drills

Drill #39: Left-Side Hitters vs. Left-Side Hitters

Objective: To set up competition against left-side hitters

Set-up: Ten players; a supply of volleyballs; a scoreboard

Description: The drill involves dividing the players into two groups, with a setter and a left side hitter on each team. Players fill in the back row to serve, pass, and play defense. One back-row player starts the drill by serving the ball over the net to the other team. The setter then sets the passed ball to the left-side hitter who attempts to score by attacking the ball against one blocker (the opposite setter) and four defenders (three back-row players and a left-side hitter). Each team is given so many opportunities to serve and attack, for example 10 balls each. The setters need to switch sides halfway through the drill to make it even for the left-side hitters.

Coaching Point: This drill is designed to establish competition among all the left-side hitters. The drill offers the left-side hitters to play their way into the starting line-up and decide who is the number 1 left-side hitter, number 2, and so on. The coach should be positioned to coach the left-side hitters during the drill. The coach can also give serving signals to the servers. The coach should make sure the volleyballs are being set far enough off the net for the attacker to take a full swing at the ball without hitting the net. Extra players can be just outside the court in the back row, ready to go in for a player in their position.

Variations: As soon as possible, this drill should be done with the left-side hitter passing and attacking the ball, if that's what they will be doing during a game. The hitter can begin to call different sets as she gets more experienced.

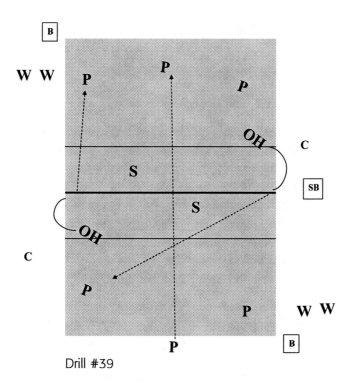

Drill #39

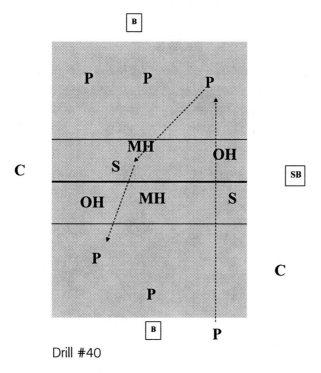

Drill #40

Drill #40: Middle Hitters vs. Middle Hitters

Objective: To set up competition against middle hitters

Set-up: All players; a supply of volleyballs; a scoreboard

Description: The drill involves dividing the players into two groups, with a setter and a middle hitter on each team. The other players fill in the court to serve, pass, and play defense. One back-row player starts the drill by serving the ball over the net to the other team. The setter then sets the passed ball to the middle hitter, who attempts to score by attacking the ball against one, two, or three blockers (left-side, middle, and setter) and three defenders in the back row. After the setter has set the ball, she attempts to help block the other middle hitter if possible. Each team is given so many opportunities to serve and attack, for example 10 balls each. The setters need to switch sides halfway through the drill to make it even for the middle hitters.

Coaching Point: This drill sets up competition among all the middle hitters. They can play their way into the starting line-up and decide who is the best middle hitter, the second best middle hitter, etc. The coach should be positioned to coach the middle hitters during the drill. The middles should be calling their sets as soon as possible to try to lose the blockers. The coach can also give serving signals to the servers. The coach should make sure the volleyballs are being set far enough off the net for the attacker to take a full swing at the ball without hitting the net. Extra players can be just outside the court in the back row, ready to go in for a player in their position.

Variations: The middle on the receiving team should be out of the service reception at first and be ready to come in strong for the attack. However, as soon as possible, the middle should be ready to pass a short serve and still come in and attack the ball and score.

Drill #41: Outside Hitters vs. Six

Objective: To match up the outside hitters against a team of six playing defense

Set-up: All players; a supply of volleyballs; a scoreboard

Description: The drill involves a team of six players positioned on one side of the net, set up in their base-defensive positions. The two outside hitters are on the other side of the net getting ready to attack the volleyball, trying to score a point. The outsides compete with one another, with each getting a certain number of swings. The scoreboard should be used to keep track of the number of attempts and kills for each player. One of the back-row players on the six-person team playing defense starts each play by serving the ball across the net to one of the passers. The ball is then passed up to the setter, who sets one of the outside hitters. The hitters rotate hitting every other ball. They should each get a certain number of attempts (e.g., 10 each). The player who gets the most points wins the drill.

Coaching Point: This drill is a good activity to help outside hitters work on killing the first ball for a point. This drill matches them up against the other outside hitters. The coach can use this drill to help determine the rank order of the outside hitters for starting line-up purposes. A coach should put her best blockers against these hitters to test their ability to score against a strong block.

Variations: The active outside hitter may also start inside the court as a passer and then go to hit. She may call out different sets to hit to try to get herself hitting against fewer blockers. This option can help illustrate the mobility of the hitters.

Drill #42: Middle Hitters vs. Six

Objective: To match up the middle hitters against a team of six playing defense

Set-up: All players; a supply of volleyballs; a scoreboard

Description: This drill involves a team of six players on one side of the net, set up in their base-defensive positions. The two middle hitters are on the other side of the net getting ready to attack the volleyball, trying to score a point. The middles compete with one another, with each getting a certain number of swings. The scoreboard should be used to track the number of attempts and kills for each player. One of the back-row players on the six-person team playing defense starts each play by serving the ball across the net to one of the passers. The ball is then passed up to the setter, who sets one of the middle hitters. The hitters rotate hitting every other ball. They each get a certain number of attempts (e.g., 10 each). The player who gets the most points wins the drill.

Coaching Point: This drill is a good activity to help middle hitters work on killing the first ball for a point. This drill matches them up against the other middle hitter. The coach can use this drill to help determine the rank order of the middle hitters for starting line-up purposes. The setters should be switched out at the halfway point of the drill, so the coach can see how the hitters connect with each setter.

Variations: The active middle hitter may also start off the net and in the attack area as a passer and then go to hit. She should pass the ball high enough that she can still make her approach to attack the ball. She may call out different sets to hit to try to get herself hitting against fewer blockers. This option can help illustrate will show the mobility of the middle hitters.

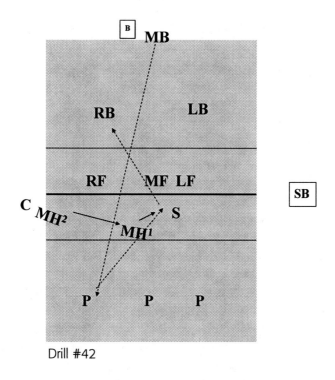

Drill #42

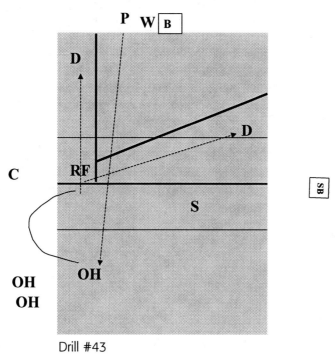

Drill #43

Drill #43: Outside-Hitter Accuracy

Objective: To help outside hitters develop the ability to hit around the blocker without making hitting errors

Set-up: Six players; a supply of volleyballs; chalk or floor tape

Description: The drill involves having three outside hitters on one side of the court, ready to pass and hit a ball from the left side of the court. A setter is positioned with them on their side of the net. Another player is on the other side of the net who will be serving to the outside hitters, while another player is positioned as the blocker. The court should be marked so that a target area is given for the hitters down the line and sharp crosscourt. The drill starts with a player serving the ball over the net to the outside hitter who is standing in the court in zone 5 or 4. The hitter then passes the served ball to the setter and approaches to hit a high outside set against a single blocker. The hitter must hit a certain number of balls (it is recommended that the coach should start with a low number, such as two) in each of the marked areas. The hitters receive a point when they hit the ball in one of those areas. If they commit a hitting error by hitting the ball into the net or out of bounds, they lose a point as a consequence for making a hitting error. They are awarded a point if the ball lands in one of the target areas or off the blocker's hands, or given a minus if they make an error and a zero if it goes in the court, but not in target area.

Coaching Point: Players need to learn how to hit around the block and into the court without making a hitting error or getting blocked. The outside hitter must concentrate on making a good pass before starting her approach to attack the set. It is also important for the hitter to land balanced on her two feet after every attack jump.

Variations: A digger can be incorporated into the drill in both the down-the-line and the sharp crosscourt target areas. While the diggers can stay in those areas to practice digging balls off a hitter, it does not matter if they dig the ball, as far as the scoring goes. Another option is to change the target areas to include short areas for tips or off-speed hits or the deep-corner crosscourt.

Drill #44: Five-Ball Drill

Objective: To train the hitters to reach high and hit the ball in the court consistently under pressure

Set-up: Five players; a supply of volleyballs

Description: The drill involves a group of three hitters, a setter, and a server on the other side of the net. The drill begins by having a player serve the ball over the net and one of the three players pass the ball to the setter (who can already be in the target zone or come in from the back row). The setter sets the ball high outside to the first outside hitter, who must hit the ball hard in the court to count as one mini-point. The other two hitters must do the same thing for it to count as one full point. The group needs to get to five full points. If one of the players commits a hitting error or the ball touches the net, the entire group goes back to zero for that point. If they have three full points and the first and second outside hitters have good hits, but the third hitter makes a hitting error or the ball touches the net, the group stays at three points.

Coaching Point: This drill is a good exercise that is designed to simulate the end of a match, when players may be tired. Hitters must hit the ball hard to count and must not be allowed to tip or off-speed a ball into the court.

Variations: Once the players can perform this drill as initially intended, the coach can designate target areas. For example, maybe only hits down the line are counted, or hits crosscourt. This option can also be done by different positions at different areas of the court, middles from the middle, and right sides from the right side of the court.

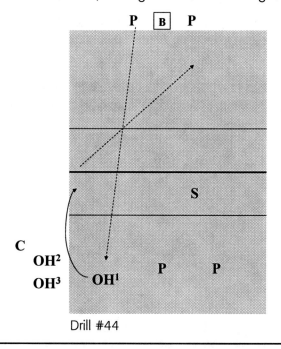

Drill #44

Drill #45: Right-Side Hitter Accuracy

Objective: To help right-side hitters develop the ability to hit around the blocker without making hitting errors

Set-up: Six players; a supply of volleyballs; chalk or floor tape

Description: The drill involves having three right-side hitters on one side of the court, ready to hit a set from the right side of the court. A setter is positioned with them on their side of the net. Players are on the other side of the net serving to extra players who then pass the serves. The drill also has a left-side blocker and a digger in each of two marked areas, one down the line and one crosscourt in right back. The court has been marked to give two target areas for the hitters. The drill begins with the ball being served to one of the passers in the back of the court. The right-side hitter starts inside the court in line with the setter and then approaches and hits a wide slide (near the antenna) or a high set a certain number of times in each marked area (it is recommended that the coach should start with a low number, such as two). If the ball goes inside the target area, the right side hitter is given a point. If the ball goes into the net, gets blocked, or goes out of bounds, the right-side hitter loses a point (as a consequence for making a hitting error.) The right-side hitters rotate around after each swing at the ball. The coach should assign someone to keep an accurate count of the number of good hits and errors in each area and to communicate the areas still needed to be hit.

Coaching Point: This drill is designed to help players learn to play the ball in the court, even if they are not given a perfect set. If they swing the same at every ball, no matter whether it is a good set or bad set or where the block is, they lose points. As a result, they should be required to keep hitting more balls at and into the targets to get themselves out of a hole.

Variations: The target areas can be changed to include short areas for tips to the middle of the court or the deep-corner crosscourt. The right-side hitter could start as a passer and then hit the set.

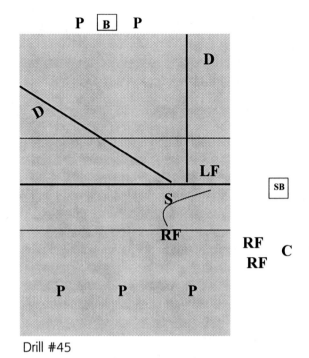

Drill #45

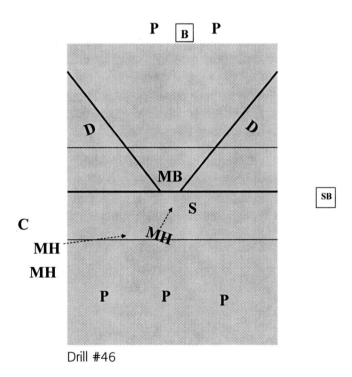

Drill #46

Drill #46: Middle-Hitter Accuracy

Objective: To help the middle hitters develop the ability to hit around a one-person block in the middle to target areas

Set-up: Six players; a supply of volleyballs; chalk or floor tape

Description: The drill involves having three middle hitters on one side of the court ready to hit a set from the middle of the court. A setter is positioned with them on their side of the net. Another player is on the other side of the net who will be serving to extra players who then pass the serves. The court should be marked, giving a target area for the hitters. The drill begins with the ball being served to one of the passers in the back of the court. The middle starts inside the attack line in a game-like position and then approaches and hits a quick set a prescribed number of times in each marked area (it is recommended that the coach should start with a low number, such as two). If the ball goes inside the target area, the middle hitter is given a point. If the ball goes into the net, gets blocked, or goes out of bounds, the middle hitter loses a point (as a consequence for making a hitting error.) The middle hitters rotate out after each swing at the ball. As such, the coach should assign someone to keep an accurate count of the number of good hits and errors in each area.

Coaching Point: Middles need to learn how to hit around the block without making a hitting error or getting blocked. This attribute is critical to being a successful middle and drawing the attention of the middle blocker away from the outside hitters in a game. The ball should be set in front of the right shoulder or left shoulder of the attacker, depending on if the middle wants to hit a power shot or a cut-back shot in front of their opposite hitting shoulder. The coach should make sure that the middle hitters are landing on both feet after jumping for every type of attack.

Variations: The target areas can be changed to include deep corners or even tips around the middle blocker. The middle hitters may also want to hit from the right side, with the target areas changed for that particular set-up (e.g., right-side hitting accuracy). Defenders could be added in the target areas to let them get some experience digging middle hitters.

Drill #47: Arm-Swing Speed

Objective: To train players to speed up their arm swing when attacking the ball

Set-up: Two players; a towel; a safe platform; a bench or bleacher

Description: This drill involves pairing up the players. One player stands on a safe platform, bench, or bleacher, so that she is taller than her partner. She drapes a towel over her shoulder and holds it out above her partner, leaving about six inches of the towel hanging down out of her hand. The player standing on the floor simulates the attack arm swing by bending her knees, and then swinging both arms back behind her and swinging both arms forward and up, before drawing the hitting arm back. She continues the swing by reaching as high as she can and hitting the towel hanging down, snapping her wrist and bringing her hand all the way down to her side. The drill should be repeated for a certain number of repetitions, such as 15 or 20.

Coaching Point: This drill provides an effective way of working on the technique of the arm swing, without the player having to jump numerous times. It is important that the player learns to complete this entire action quickly, if she wants to learn to hit the ball hard when spiking. Initially, the drill can be performed at a relatively slow speed. However, as soon as the player's technique is correct, she should swing full speed for every repetition, snapping the towel.

Variations: This drill can be done near the net, so the player has the feeling of how far she needs to be from the net so she can take a hard swing at the ball and not hit the net.

Drill #48: Left Side to Left Side

Objective: To provide left-side players with the experience of passing and hitting, as well as digging and hitting a high outside set

Set-up: Eight players; a supply of volleyballs; a scoreboard

Description: The drill starts out with a server (middle back or left back) serving the ball over the net. One of the players passes the volleyball up to the setter/right side, who then sets the ball high outside for the left-side hitter. She then hits it over the net crosscourt towards the left side (zone 4 or 5) on the other court. The setter and the other players should move in to cover the hitter and then move back to their defensive positions to get ready to be attacked by the other team's left side.

Coaching Point: The coach should make sure that the outside hitter stays up at the net in a blocking position, before backing off the net to get ready to dig the hitter. Players also may need to be reminded to cover their hitter before getting in their defensive positions. Because the left sides are in zone 4 of the court, the drill could also be called 4-to-4.

Variations: A variation of this drill may be to have the left sides spike roll (standing on the ground using an overhead hitting motion) the ball over to the opposite left side. This drill could be used as a warm-up at the beginning of practice. After the players are warmed up, they can jump and off-speed the ball over the net toward the left-side attacker. Finally, the drill can go full speed, with both left-side hitters taking full swings at the volleyball, trying to get a kill. Another variation is to switch and run this drill for the right sides or 2-to-2.

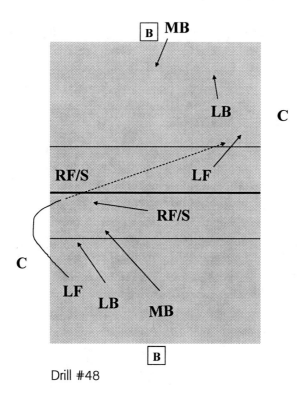

Drill #48

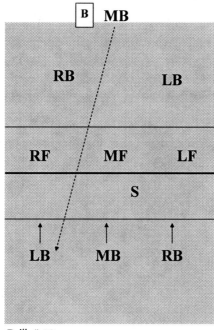

Drill #49

Drill #49: Back-Row Attack vs. Team Defense

Objective: To teach players how to hit a set as a back-row player and how to defend against it

Set-up: All players; a supply of volleyballs

Description: This drill involves having three players start in their back-row positions, with a setter on their side of the net. The ball is introduced to the side of the net with the back-row players, who then pass the ball up to their setter. As the setter is getting ready to set the ball (only antenna-height or 10 feet), all three back-row players begin their attack approach and call the name of the set to their area of the court (A, C, Pipe, etc.). Although the setter will be facing the left-front area of the court, she should set the ball laterally antenna-height, so it lands slightly in front of the attack line. The back-row player to whom the ball is set finishes the approach she has already began by taking off behind the attack line, hitting the ball, and landing in front of the attack line. The middle on the opposite side of the net tries to block the attack. The three defenders behind the blocker move from their base position when the ball is set to their defensive positions, deep in the court around the blocker. They then dig the ball up to the middle of the court. As their setter contacts the ball, they begin their approach to hit the ball around the opposing middle blocker. Each side receives a certain number of attempts to score. The team with the most points wins the drill.

Coaching Point: The coach should make sure that all players eligible to attack out of the back row are beginning their approach early enough so that the ball can be set low, in an attempt to keep a double-block from forming. The middle blocker should be reminded to be careful not to reach too far outside her body to try to block the ball. She may end up deflecting the ball out of the reach of her back-row players.

Variations: The setter should be allowed to dump the ball or set the back row to keep the back-row defense honest (e.g., staying in their base positions until the ball is set to the back-row player).

Drill #50: Attack Approach with a Tennis Ball

Objective: To help attackers learn to use both arms in their backswing during the attack approach

Set-up: One player; one tennis ball

Description: The player starts at or near the attack line, with a tennis ball in her non-hitting hand (her left hand if the player hits with her right hand). As she begins her approach toward the net, she should swing her arms back on her second step. She then moves the ball to her hitting hand. As both arms swing forward, she jumps near the net, simulating an attack, during which she throws the tennis ball over the net into the opposite court.

Coaching Point: This drill is designed to train players to use both arms in a full backswing to give them a faster approach and higher jump when spiking.

Variations: The players may do this from different areas along the net or in the back row, learning how to hit various parts of the court or different angles.

Drill #51: Attacking Around the Block

Objective: To help attackers learn to see the blocker's hands

Set-up: All players; a swimming pool noodle cut in half; a supply of volleyballs

Description: The drill involves having one player in a blocking position at the net, who will block during the hitting drill. The only difference is that the player will be holding up a half noodle in each hand. They can block the line, block crosscourt, or leave a hole in the block. The hitter should be able to see the bright colored noodles and learn to hit around them or through the hole.

Coaching Point: This drill is a great way to get the hitter to see the block out of her peripheral vision. The bright colored noodles can be held in various positions as the attacker is approaching the net to hit the set. Obviously, even if the ball hits the noodle, no damage will occur to anything or anyone.

Variations: Another blocker could be added to the drill, so that the attacker will see four noodles, simulating the four hands of the blocker, and will learn to hit around them to avoid being blocked.

Drill #52: Attacker Target Hitting

Objective: To develop the ability of attackers to hit a variety of shots and to place the ball in different areas of the court, depending on what is open

Set-up: Five players; chalk or floor tape; a supply of volleyballs

Description: The drill involves marking target areas on the opposite court (e.g., an area in the opposite deep corner, an area down the line, an area sharp crosscourt, an area inside the block, and an area in the middle of the court). One of the outside hitters receives a serve from another player. She then passes the ball to her setter, who sets her. The objective of the drill is to have each player score by hitting a ball in each one of these zones, as well as a ball hit off the blocker's hands out of bounds. The next hitter then steps into the court to receive her serve.

Coaching Point: The coach should assign someone to keep track of the target zones each player hits. That designee should let the players know what zones they still need to hit to complete the drill.

Variations: This same drill could also be done for the middle and right-side hitters, placing the targets in zones that will be weaknesses in their opponent's defense that they will most likely need to attack during a game. Based on the skill level of the players, the drill can be changed by moving the target zones and increasing the required number of balls to be hit off the blocker's hands.

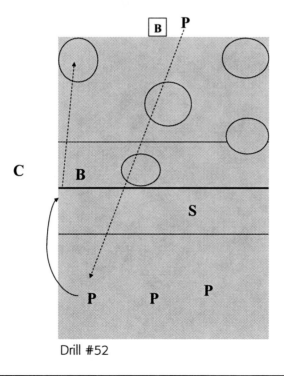

Drill #52

Drill #53: Repetitive Attacks

Objective: To help attackers learn to transition off the net repeatedly and make strong approaches each time

Set-up: All players; a supply of volleyballs

Description: The drill begins with a ball coming over the net to a player in the front row, who then passes it to the setter. The setter sets the ball for that attacker to hit. Another ball then comes over the net for the player to pass and hit. This pattern continues until everyone has passed and hit three balls in a row over the net into the opposite court successfully.

Coaching Point: After each successful attack, the player should turn and get herself back to the attack line, while keeping her eye on the ball coming over the net. She then moves to pass and attack the next ball.

Variations: All factors considered, the number of times a player is able to properly pass and hit the ball as intended in this drill is dependent almost entirely on her skill level. As the player gets more skilled, that number will increase. The hitter can eventually move along the net, hitting a variety of sets.

Drill #54: Attacking Self-Toss

Objective: To help players learn the timing needed for hitting a ball, as well as learning the movements for a jump serve

Set-up: Two players; two volleyballs

Description: The drill involves pairing up the players. One player is at the attack line with a volleyball. She begins the drill by underhand tossing (with topspin) the volleyball up near the net with her hitting hand. She then immediately begins her attack approach and jumps and hits the ball straight ahead over the net into the other court. Her partner rolls her a second ball, while she retrieves the first ball. The partners should switch roles after hitting 10 good balls into the court successfully.

Coaching Point: This drill may take the players a while to learn both how to toss the ball properly with topspin near the net and the timing of the approach to hit it with power over the net and into the court. Once they learn this technique, this drill can be an excellent warm-up exercise for hitting or learning to jump serve. The coach should strongly emphasize that the partner should not roll the ball back when a player is getting ready to jump and hit another ball.

Variations: The player can continue to move back from the net until she is starting behind the endline. Players can develop a powerful jump serve, using this progression.

Drill #55: Keep Away

Objective: To learn to hit the ball away from certain players

Set-up: Three players; a supply of volleyballs

Description: The drill involves having one player serve the ball to a player, who then passes the ball to the setter, who sets the ball to an attacker. The server moves somewhere around the court. The attacker must hit the ball away from that player.

Coaching Point: This drill is designed to help the attackers be aware of player positioning on the other side of the court.

Variations: Additional players can be added to the drill as blockers and more defensive players. This option could be applied in a six-on-six scrimmage, with one player having on a special color shirt. The goal of the game is to keep that player from touching the first ball over the net, such as a serve, an attack, or a free ball.

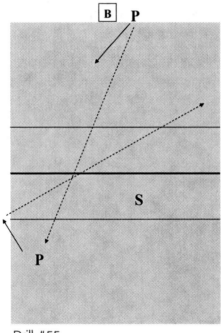

Drill #55

6

Blocking Drills

Drill #56: Blocking Gloves

Objective: To help players learn what their hands are doing in blocking drills

Set-up: Two players; a supply of volleyballs; a pair of bright work gloves

Description: This drill involves two-person groups, setting up in a basic blocking position, with bright gloves on their hands. The players then go through the motions of the blocking drill, without an actual ball involved, to let them see what their hands are doing. Next, a player or coach can stand on a safe hitting platform and toss a ball into the air and hit the ball into the blocker's hands. The player blocking should direct the ball back into the court by the way their hands are facing.

Coaching Point: This drill is designed to help players learn to see their hands out of their peripheral vision, primarily because their gloves are so bright. If the hands drop too low in the blocking-ready position or the hands drop back away from the net, the blocker will lose sight of their hands.

Variations: The players could use the gloves in a more complex drill against live setters and hitters.

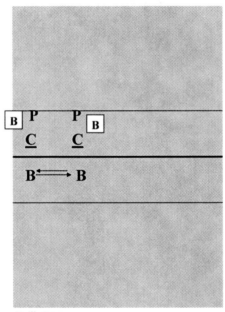

Drill #56

Drill #57: Blocking –
Right Hand, Left Hand, Both Hands

Objective: To teach players that they need to be equally strong with both hands and shoulders when blocking

Set-up: Two players; a supply of volleyballs; a safe hitting platform

Description: The drill involves pairing up the players. One player is in a ready blocking position at the net. She jumps up and penetrates the net with only her right hand to block the ball down into the court. Her partner has a ball and is positioned on a safe hitting platform across the net. She then tosses the ball up in the air and hits into the right hand the blocker has placed over the net. Once that player has blocked five balls down into the court with her right hand, she continues the drill, blocking only with her left hand. Once she has blocked five balls down into the court with only her left hand, she then continues the drill, blocking five balls down into the court with both hands.

Coaching Point: The area should be kept clear of extra volleyballs rolling around on the floor, so it will be safe for the blockers jumping. The coach should make sure to have the player blocking line up in front of the shoulder of the person hitting the ball.

Variations: This same drill can be done with the players wearing "blocking gloves."

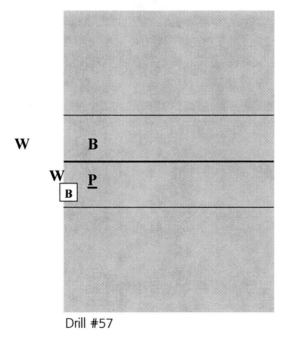

Drill #57

Drill #58: Ten Blocks in a Row

Objective: To train players to keep their hands high and to be ready to get them over the net as quickly as possible when moving along the net

Set-up: Five players; two baskets of balls; two safe-hitting platforms

Description: The drill involves having two people (coaches or players) on safe-hitting platforms on one side of the net, with one near the sideline and the other a few steps inside the court. One player is behind each of them, handing volleyballs to them, as needed. The player in the blocking drill is positioned across the net from one of the attackers. The person on the box, near the antennae, tosses the ball up and hits the ball into the blocker's hands. As soon as the ball is blocked, the next person on the box further inside the court then tosses the ball up and hits it into the blocker's hands. The blocker moves as quickly as possible from side to side, trying to front the hitter's shoulder to successfully block the ball down. It is important for the blocker to keep her hands above her head, so that she can get her hands across the net quickly. She should land in a flexed position with her hands still high, taking a shuffle step or crossover step to get to the next hitter. She goes back and forth, attempting to block 10 balls in a row.

Coaching Point: The coach may want to stand behind the blocker with her hands under the player's elbows to help her keep her from dropping her hands below head height. This step allows the player to be ready to block quick multiple attacks at the net, such as a quick middle attack and then a slide. The blocker should be careful to avoid swinging her elbows.

Variations: The outside blockers should work on this drill from the outside to inside the middle-third of the court. The middle blockers should work on this drill in the middle-third of the court.

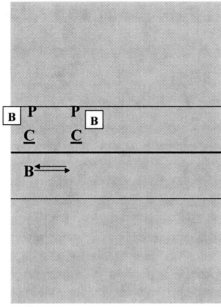

Drill #58

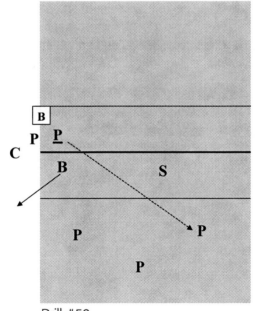

Drill #59

Drill #59: Block and Attack

Objective: To train players to land properly on a block and transition off the net to prepare to attack the ball

Set-up: Five players; a supply of volleyballs; a safe-hitting platform

Description: This drill involves positioning one blocker at the net, opposite another player who is on a safe-hitting platform. A setter and three defensive players are on the court with the blocker. The player on the platform tosses the ball up and hits the ball into the court. The blocker can block the ball for a point. If the ball goes by the blocker to one of the diggers, the blocker will follow the ball with her eyes and turn to transition off the net to the attack line. The setter then steps in to set the dug ball to the attacker. If the attacker hits the ball into the court, she scores a point. In order to score a point, the blocker must block the ball or transition off the net and successfully attack the dug ball. This drill can be conducted for any position in the front row along the net. The drill ends when the blocker either blocks or transitions properly and hits three balls into the court.

Coaching Point: This drill is a good exercise to allow the coach to watch the blocker's eyes to make sure she keeps them open while blocking and then turns her head the direction the ball goes by her. This step will help her learn to watch the ball and get off the net quickly to the attack line, if possible, and then begin her attack approach. The coach should also make sure the blocker is landing balanced on both feet when blocking and attacking.

Variations: This drill can be set up to have the blocker audible or call out the set she wants to attack, so she can learn to communicate with the setter. A defensive back row can be added to dig the ball the blocker transitioned to hit over. The number of successful attempts can also be varied, based on the skill level of the players.

Drill #60: Blocking Multiple Attackers

Objective: To help the middle blocker learn to see all the hitters along the net and move to block them

Set-up: All players; a supply of volleyballs; five safe-hitting platforms

Description: The drill involves having a team of six players on one side of the net, preparing to set a block and play defense against one of the five hitters on the other court on the safe platforms at the net. A coach stands behind the team of six so they cannot see her. The coach then points to one of the hitters on the box. That player tosses the ball up at least three feet and hits it into the court at the six players. The front row needs to be alert and move to the attacker who tosses the ball as quickly as possible in order to attempt to block her. The drill continues until five balls are blocked.

Coaching Point: The player on the box who is directed to hit the ball should toss the ball high enough to give the middle blocker a fair chance to move and get in front of that hitter. This drill is designed to improve the blocker's vision along the net and her reaction and movement time.

Variations: This drill could first be run with two outside hitters on boxes, so that the team learns the drill. Another hitter on a box could be added to the drill until there are five options along the net. Three other players could be positioned on boxes in the back row, who could also serve as attackers.

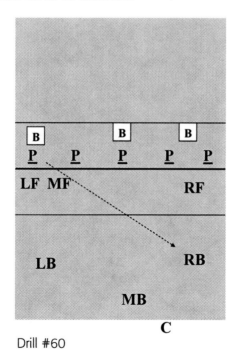

Drill #60

Drill #61: Blocking with Bracelets

Objective: To train players to use a maximum jump each time they block

Set-up: One player; two silicone bracelets or wristbands

Description: The drill involves having one player at the net working on blocking jumps or her blocking steps with a jump. She should have a silicone bracelet (breast cancer, livestrong, etc.) or wristband on each arm at the position where her arms cross the top of the net when blocking using a maximum jump. The player should perform 10 block jumps, with the bracelets reaching the top of the net each time.

Coaching Point: It is important to properly determine how high the player can jump and get their hands or arms across the net to block. The bracelets should be placed at this area and kept there.

Variations: Sweatbands could also be used for this drill. The players could keep the bracelets or sweatbands on when they perform other blocking drills with live hitters or for a six-on-six scrimmage to see if they can keep their block jump at the same level the entire game or match.

Drill #62: Peer Coaching Blockers

Objective: To help players learn to see the correct technique needed when blocking

Set-up: Four players; a safe-hitting platform; a supply of volleyballs

Description: A player is on a safe-hitting platform at the net, with a supply of volleyballs being handed to her. A blocker is at the net, ready to jump and block the ball being tossed and hit by the player on the box. Another player (a peer) is standing off the court to the side, observing the technique of the blocker. The peer gives feedback to the blocker, telling her what she is doing well and what she needs to do differently to block more balls.

Coaching Point: This drill allows the players to teach each other—a process that can help improve their technique as well, since they can see what each other is doing. Being able to teach something can help improve their understanding of the skill. The coach should make sure that the peers are telling their teammates what they need to do, instead of telling them what they are doing wrong.

Variations: A double-block could be added to the drill, with two peers each helping one of the blockers. Middles could watch other middles, with outside blockers peer mentoring other outside blockers. Then, middles could serve as the peer coach for the outsides, while the outsides serve as the peer coach for the middles.

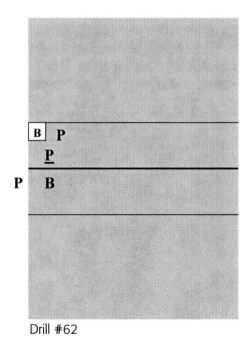

Drill #62

Drill #63: Blocking Zones at the Net

Objective: To help players learn to keep their hands high at the net, while moving to block quick sets hit by two different players

Set-up: Five players; two safe-hitting platforms; a supply of volleyballs; two ball baskets

Description: The drill involves having left-side player start in front of one player on a box with the ball. That player tosses the ball and tries to hit it past the blocker. The player attempts to block the ball back into the opposite court. Immediately upon the blocker landing, the other player on a box tosses a ball, and the blocker must quickly move to position herself in front of that attacker's hitting arm to try to block the ball. This drill continues until the player has blocked a certain number of balls. The players hitting the volleyballs should be in various positions on boxes along the net to simulate where a setter and a right-side hitter might hit the ball.

Coaching Point: A left-side blocker is responsible for being ready to block a right-side hitter, the setter, or a middle hitter approaching to hit a slide on the right side of the court. The blocker should keep her hands high to reduce the time it takes to get her hands across the net to block the ball. The blocker also needs to make sure to land balanced on both feet each time to help prevent being injured and to make sure she is ready to change direction quickly.

Variations: As the players get better, the attackers on boxes may be moved farther apart, providing an even greater challenge to the blocker to cover more of the net. Initially, this drill should be done for middle blockers moving along the middle third of the net and then for right-side blockers who need to be able to block from the antennae to the position where a shoot-set may be attacked by the middle.

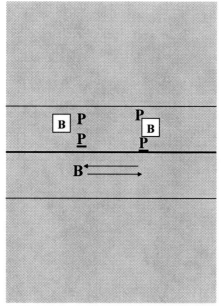

Drill #63

Drill #64: Blocking Hat

Objective: To train blockers to keep their eyes on the attacker when they are approaching to hit the ball

Set-up: All players; a supply of volleyballs; a baseball hat

Description: A blocker at the net wears a baseball hat. Another player serves the ball from behind the endline to a passer on the other side of the net. To start the drill, the ball is passed to a setter, who sets to the attacker opposite the blocker with the hat. The blocker watches the hitter and attempts to block the ball.

Coaching Point: This drill is designed to force the blocker to watch the flight of the ball for a short time after it leaves the setter's hands and then turn to watch the attacker and line up with her approach to block the hitter. If the player tries to watch the ball too long, the bill of the hat will block her vision.

Variations: The entire front row of blockers could wear hats in a scrimmage situation to train them to focus on the hitter after the ball has been set.

7

Digging Drills

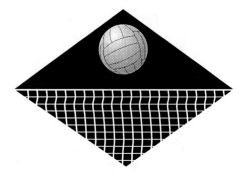

Drill #65: Dig and Attack

Objective: To teach players to concentrate first on a successful dig to the setter or middle of the court and then begin their attack approach

Set-up: All players; a supply of volleyballs

Description: The drill involves having two full teams on the court. The ball can be attacked over the net at any of the players for them to dig up. The players need to make sure they are reading the attacker (i.e., see which way they are looking) and then make a good dig to the middle of the court. The ball should be dug up high enough to allow them to make a good strong approach to attack the ball successfully around the block. The setter should set the ball to the player who just dug up the ball. If it is the libero, they can still attack—spike roll or drive the ball over the net, standing on the ground making sure the ball is contacted below the top of the net.

Coaching Point: This drill is designed to increase the accuracy of the dig, so that the attacker has enough time to take a strong approach to hit. It also helps make sure that after a player digs the ball, she will be moving forward to an attacking ready position.

Variations: This drill can also be done to improve the attacking readiness of the back-row players.

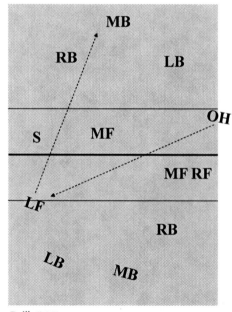

Drill #65

Drill #66: Defense Using One Volleyball

Objective: To help players understand that they need to make an attempt to play every ball

Set-up: All players; one volleyball.

Description: The coach can run whatever defensive drill she wants to with the team; however, only one volleyball will be used. When the coach hits the volleyball and it is dug back to the target or to the coach, the drill continues. If it is dug off the court or if the ball hits the floor and goes off the court without being touched, the entire team has to go get the ball and bring it back to the coach. This drill can continue until the team learns to give a full defensive effort for the ball every time.

Coaching Point: Most of the time, coaches have baskets of numerous volleyballs for their use to hit at players to practice defense. The players get so used to another ball being hit at them, that they sometimes don't focus as much as they should on every ball. This drill puts the focus on digging up every volleyball—just like in a game. The coach should make sure to put the rest of the volleyballs out of sight during this drill.

Variations: This drill could also be done with a limited number of volleyballs, thereby emphasizing the importance of the one ball in play.

Drill #67: Partner Digs Toward the Net

Objective: To help players learn the distance to the net and develop the ability to dig the ball without hitting it

Set-up: All players; one volleyball needed for every two players

Description: The drill involves pairing up the players. One player is five feet from the net. The drill begins when she tosses the ball up to herself and hits it at her partner 20 feet away from the net. The partner digs the ball up to the player at the net, who then hits it down at her again. The drill continues until the ball is dug up to her partner 10 times.

Coaching Point: It is important to always practice digging toward the net, so the players understand the size of the court and how to keep the ball on their own side of the net.

Variations: Each player may contact the ball twice. The player at the net tosses the ball and hits it to her partner, who digs it up to the net. That player can then set the ball to herself, allowing the back-row partner to move to her base on the court and then transition back to dig the next ball.

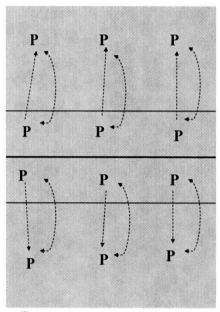

Drill #67

Drill #68: Two Minutes

Objective: To help train players to go for every ball

Set-up: Two players; a supply of volleyballs

Description: The drill involves having two players start out on the court playing defense against the coach or a player who hits balls at them. The coach, standing on the ground on the same side of the net, tosses a ball to herself and then hits the ball toward one of the players. That player digs the ball up, while the other player transitions up and sets the ball back to the coach. She needs to set the ball high enough so that she and her partner can back up to their defensive position and be stopped and ready to dig that ball from the coach. This drill continues for two minutes. The drill starts over if a player does not make an attempt to make a defensive play on the ball.

Coaching Point: This drill provides an opportunity for the two defensive players to read the "hitter," dig a ball up, and have their partner step in to set the second ball. It also forces the players to keep backing up to their position each time, just as they need to do in a game. The coach can regulate the difficulty of this drill by hitting at or near the players, or she can force the players to extend their defensive coverage. The players need to understand the angles of pursuit when the ball is hit between them. The player closest to the hitter goes in front, while the player furthest away from the hitter goes behind. The coach should move along the net so the players receive hits from all areas.

Variations: A third player could be added to this drill as a defensive player. In such a scenario, some communication needs to occur between the players, regarding which one will set the second ball and where they will back up to on defense. A setter could be added as another player.

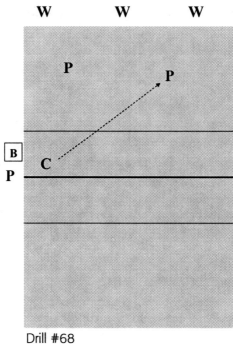

Drill #68

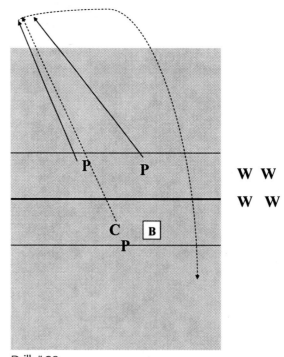

Drill #69

Drill #69: Off-Court Saves

Objective: To help players understand a system for saving the volleyball that has been passed or dug off the court

Set-up: Two players; a coach; a supply of volleyballs

Description: The drill involves having two players stand at the net, with the coach on the other side of the net. The drill begins when the coach throws the ball out of bounds past the endline. The two players run to retrieve the ball and get it back over the net. The first player to get to the ball passes it straight up above herself. The second player then steps in, getting her body in a balanced position, with her back and shoulders square to the net. She sends the ball high enough to go over the net and into the opponent's court.

Coaching Point: It is important for a strategy to exist to get this type of errant pass or dig back over the net. Communication between the players is important. The second player getting to the ball should be reminding the first player to "get it straight up" and to let her know she has enough room to play the ball without running into the wall, seating, or other objects that would be unsafe. During a game situation, all six players should be pursuing the volleyball in an attempt to save it. Obviously, the person who just played it in that direction cannot be the next person to contact it. She could, however, be the person who sends it back over the net.

Variations: This drill can be done with more than two players, thereby increasing the necessity for communication.

Drill #70: Three vs. Middle Hit

Objective: To help players learn to dig a middle hitter, keep the ball in play, and communicate, while getting the ball back over the net

Set-up: Four players; a safe-hitting platform; a supply of volleyballs

Description: The drill involves having three players on the court in their back-row defensive positions. Another player is on a stable hitting platform, on the opposite side of the net in the middle of the court. That player tosses a ball up and hits it over the net at or near one of the three players. All three players must contact the ball before it goes over the net. As a result, if player #1 digs the volleyball, then players #2 or #3 must set the ball to the remaining player who has not contacted the ball. That final player should jump and attack the ball over the net and into the opposing court. This drill continues until the players have dug, set, and hit a certain number of volleyballs successfully over the net and into the court.

Coaching Point: The coach should make sure that the other players not involved in the drill are kept busy keeping all the volleyballs out of the way or digging up the attacked ball on the hitter's side of the court. The drill should be conducted in such a way to keep everyone moving. For example, if the defense digs the ball, another player needs to catch it and put it back in the ball basket.

Variations: This drill could be done with four players, with the extra player serving as a blocker at the net.

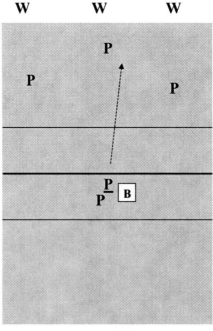

Drill #70

Drill #71: Defensive Movements with a Reaction Ball (Z ball)

Objective: To develop eye-hand coordination, the ability to stay low, and first-step quickness to the ball on defense

Set-up: All players; a supply of reaction balls

Description: The team is divided into two-person groups, with each set of partners given one reaction ball. The players can be scattered around the court. One partner tosses the reaction ball (or Z ball) up in the air near her partner. That player lets the ball bounce twice and then tries to catch it. Offering an excellent way to get the players moving, this drill is an activity that could, for example be done for five minutes before performing a defensive drill. The partners who catch the most number of balls during that time are the winners.

Coaching Point: Reaction balls can be purchased from fitness or training stores. A reaction ball is a hard rubber, odd-shaped ball that bounces randomly. If the ball only bounces once, it has a more predictable bounce and is not too hard to catch. Letting the ball bounce twice gives it a random bounce, which results in players really having to be ready to react to it quickly to catch it.

Variations: Coaches can experiment with the height of the toss to challenge the players. The ball could be tossed over the net, with three players in the back row trying to catch the ball after the second bounce.

Drill #72: Coach Under the Net Run-Throughs

Objective: To help players learn to stay low and accelerate to play a ball and back up quickly

Set-up: All players; a supply of volleyballs

Description: To start the drill, the coach kneels under the net at the centerline (using a towel or kneepad for padding) and tosses a volleyball to each of three players, positioned with one on the right back endline, another at the middle of the court endline, and the third player on the left back endline. The coach tosses the ball low enough near the attack line that the player will need to sprint in a low position to pass the ball to a target who is standing near the middle of the court close to the net. After passing the ball, the player quickly retreats back to the endline and waits for the coach to toss to the other two players, before receiving her next toss. The players should stay in the drill until their partner standing behind them has counted five good passes to the target for them. That player can then be replaced and count for another player.

Coaching Point: The partners should count out loud so that the coach knows how many good passes each player has made. The coach controls how tough this drill is by the speed she moves from one toss to the next. The players should stay on their feet at all times during this drill. Falling to the ground to play a ball will not allow them to be back in place at the endline for their next toss. Each player should complete the drill in two different positions, based on where they play during a game.

Variations: This drill can by changed by increasing the number of good passes each player is expected to make. The coach can also vary where the players are along the net. For example, instead of being in the middle of the court under the net, they may be on the right side or left side of the court.

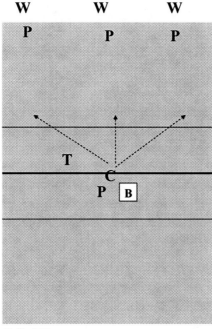

Drill #72

Drill #73: Pancake Game

Objective: To teach players how low the ball can be to the floor to still play it up legally

Set-up: All players; a supply of volleyballs

Description: The players are divided into groups of five. Each group forms a circle. One of the players in the circle tosses the volleyball up near one of the other players. The player nearest the ball after it bounces once then pancakes the ball. Each of the other players see how many of them can play the ball with a pancake before the ball goes dead.

Coaching Point: This drill is a fun activity for players to do, while waiting for practice to begin or during a break in practice.

Variations: The number of players in the group can vary from one player doing this exercise by herself to the entire team trying to see if they can all pancake this one ball before it goes out of play.

Drill #74: Dig and Cover

Objective: To help players learn to control their defensive digs

Set-up: Two players; one volleyball

Description: The drill involves dividing the players into two-person groups. One player is given the ball and is positioned inside the attack line five feet from the net, while her partner is about 20 feet away from the net. The player at the net with the ball sets the ball to herself and hits the ball down at her partner who then digs the ball back up to her near the net and moves forward to touch her partner, before quickly retreating to her position. Next, the player at the net sets the dig to herself and then hits the ball to her partner again. This drill should be done for 10 repetitions in a row without missing, before the partners switch places.

Coaching Point: The coach should make sure defensive players are digging towards the net. It is essential that they learn the court dimensions and understand to always dig the ball on their own side of the net during a game.

Variations: The defensive player could dig the ball straight up to herself and then overhand set the ball back to the hitter near the net.

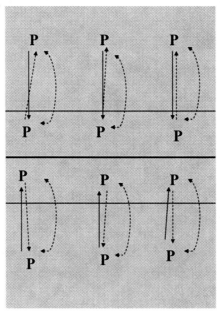

Drill #74

Drill #75: Overhead Digging

Objective: To train players to have strong hands to play a hard-hit ball overhead

Set-up: Two players; one volleyball

Description: The drill involves having two players positioned 15-to-20 feet from one another inside the volleyball court, playing pepper (alternating hitting, digging, and setting the ball). Instead of hitting the ball down at her partner's arms, the player making the hit should aim for her partner's shoulders or above. The player receiving the hit should get her hands up, with her fingers spread and her wrists stiff. At that point, she should try to set the ball straight up in the air. The ball should be hit off speed, until the defender feels comfortable with receiving a harder hit. The players should be able to dig 10 balls to their partner or a target using the overhead dig or set.

Coaching Point: The coach should make sure players understand to open their hands wide, with their fingers and thumbs spread to help make a fairly flat surface with which to contact the ball. It is important for the players to be in a position on the court so that they are only digging balls overhead that would still land in the court. They could move up in their defensive positions on the court if they learn to dig overhead successfully.

Variations: As the players improve their overhead digging skills, they could be required to use overhead digs in certain positions on the court in any of the various defensive drills that a team employs.

Drill #76: Defense vs. Coach

Objective: To train players to learn to read the hitter and be ready for all types of hits

Set-up: Three players; a supply of volleyballs

Description: The drill involves having three players in their defensive positions in the back row of the court. Standing on the ground on the same side of the net, the coach tosses a ball to herself and hits it at one of the three defenders. The ball is dug up, and one of the other players steps in and sets the ball back to the coach. The players immediately back up into their defensive position, ready to dig the next ball. The ball can be hit hard, off speed, or tipped. The coach should also move freely along the net to challenge the defense and make the person setting the ball back to her find where she is. The drill continues until the players have successfully dug and set a certain number of balls back to the coach. The primary goal of the drill is to keep the ball in play.

Coaching Point: Defensive players should begin in their base position, read, and move to the best position on the court to dig the ball being hit. They should also communicate where they think the ball is going to be hit by "reading" the way the hitter is looking. The players also need to communicate who needs to step in and set the dug ball. The players may need to switch positions, based on where they end up after setting the ball, so the court stays balanced.

Variations: Another player can be added to the drill as a setter to set every second ball back to the coach. Yet another player could be added to have four defensive players (off blocker) and a setter.

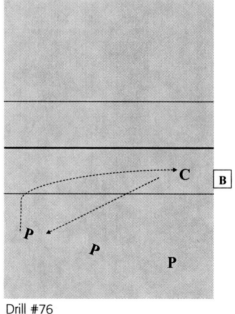

Drill #76

Drill #77: Net Recovery

Objective: To teach players a system to use to successfully play a volleyball hit into the net

Set-up: Two players; a supply of volleyballs

Description: The drill involves dividing the players into two-person groups. One partner stands near the net, while her partner stands at least 10 feet away, with a ball. The player with the ball throws the ball into the net at various speeds and trajectories. The player at the net watches the ball go into the net and then passes it up to their partner, so she can play it over the net on the next hit. The two players should be able to play the ball off the net and hit it over the net 10 times before switching positions.

Coaching Point: The players need to learn that if the ball hits the net near the bottom, it will bounce out further than if it contacts the net near the top, where it will likely fall more straight down closer to the net. Coaches should let the players experiment with this attribute of the ball and see for themselves how differently the ball will come out of the net, based on the speed, area of the net, and trajectory of the ball.

Variations: This type of activity could be used to start any of the six-on-six drills, instead of always starting a drill sending a ball over the net with a serve or free ball.

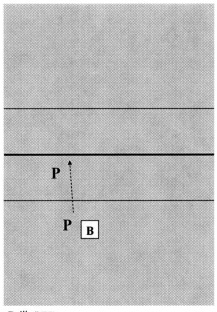

Drill #77

8

Team-Offense Drills

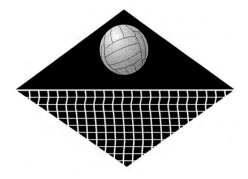

Drill #78: Three-Out-of-Five Serve Receive

Objective: To put pressure on the starting team to win the rally three-out-of-five attempts against the second team

Set-up: All players; a supply of volleyballs; a scoreboard

Description: The drill starts by having the second team serve to the starting team in their serve-reception formation. They receive the serve and run their offense against a full-team defense. The rally is played out to its natural conclusion. It is expected the first team should be able to score at least three out of five times. The losing team should have some type of consequence to keep the pressure on both teams. The consequences may be having to do a predetermined number of calisthenics, such as sit-ups, push-ups, or a few sprints…just enough to make them a little uncomfortable and push harder to win the next set of rallies. When one team wins, that team rotates. The drill should end when the first team has rotated all the way around.

Coaching Point: This drill is a good exercise to equalize both teams. When the situation arises, the second team always enjoys watching the first team fulfill its consequences when it loses.

Variations: The numbers can be changed or adapted to the level of play. If time in practice is limited, the starting team can work on their three weakest rotations or on a reception pattern they may have trouble with during a match.

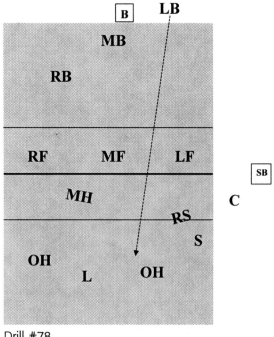

Drill #78

Drill #79: Team Serve-Receive to 30 Points

Objective: To learn how important it is to have a good pass to the setter in order to have options on offense

Set-up: All players; a supply of volleyballs; a scoreboard

Description: This drill will start with players serving to the passers (three) on the court. Whoever passes the ball then steps off the court and lets another player come in to replace her in the serve-reception. Add a setter to set the ball to the left-side position, where a player catches the ball. The coach or manager uses a scoreboard to keep track of each perfect pass and reward one point for each one. If the pass goes over the net or if it is an ace serve, three points are subtracted from the total. Eventually, the coach can begin to add more skills to this drill. For example, one of the passers could be required to hit the ball set to the left side. Then, a blocker could be added against the left-side hitter. Other options are to add a middle hitter, then a middle blocker against her, then some diggers in the back row, etc. The goal of the drill is to make 30 perfect passes, with a penalty enforced for passing the ball over the net or being aced.

Coaching Point: The coach or another player can give a signal to the servers. The coach should monitor the aggressiveness of the serves, so the players can't ease off on their teammates. If the serve is not tough enough, then the play is a wash with no point given.

Variations: This drill can be done for an entire practice. With the addition of more players and skills, it can develop into a six-on-six drill. Remember, the goal is still to get 30 good passes to the target.

Drill #80: Weakest Rotations

Objective: To allow the team to work on serve-reception rotations, which appear to be weak and allow too many points

Set-up: All players; a supply of volleyballs; a scoreboard

Description: This drill is run as a six-on-six scrimmage. The teams do not rotate. Instead, they stay in one of the weak rotations until they earn a certain number of points. One team continues to serve to the receiving team, and they play the ball out to its natural conclusion before serving another ball to the receiving team.

Coaching Point: Coaches can determine their three weakest rotations by looking at the score sheet and calculating the points made and lost per rotation. This drill allows the team to work on the rotations that need the extra time and focus for improvement.

Variations: Coaches could also decide to focus on their three strongest rotations, making sure they score lots of points while they're in these top three rotations.

Drill #81: Score on First Swing

Objective: To teach the importance of receiving the serve and scoring on the first swing or attack

Set-up: All players; a supply of volleyballs; a scoreboard

Description: This drill involves a scrimmage, with a point only being given when the team scores on the first swing after they receive the serve. The ball can be played out, but a point is only scored if there is a kill on the first play.

Coaching Point: This drill is a good activity to isolate a player who needs to work on hitting under pressure. This drill can be done with various players at different times.

Variations: The coach can call out the name of one player who has to score on the first swing or ball, thereby putting extra pressure on a player who needs to be able to put the ball away.

Drill #82: Out-of-System Attacking

Objective: To help attackers learn to adjust their approach when the ball is being set to them from the back court

Set-up: All players; a supply of volleyballs

Description: On one side of the net, there should be an outside attacker on the left side of the court and a right-side attacker on the right side of the court. Three other players are in left, middle, and right back. To begin the drill, the coach tosses the ball to one of the players in the back row, who then calls out the player's name to whom she is setting in the front row crosscourt from where she is positioned. She sets the ball so that it drops five feet off the net and five feet inside the antenna or sideline. The attacker then hits the ball into the opposite court. The players in the back row are playing defense against those two attackers. Once the ball is dug up, that ball should be caught, and another ball is tossed to the back row to set. This drill lasts until each team hits a certain number of balls successfully into the opponent's court. The players should rotate to make sure that they get to play in the positions they play in a game in both the front and back row.

Coaching Point: It is important for the players to communicate to whom they are setting the ball, so that no confusion exists concerning who is supposed to hit their set. It also forces the players to look down to see who their attacker is. The target is off the net and inside the court, so there is no chance for the ball to accidentally be set over the net or on top of it. The set should allow the attacker to take a good swing at the ball without hitting the net.

Variations: A blocker can be added against the hitters, so they must hit around them to hit into the court.

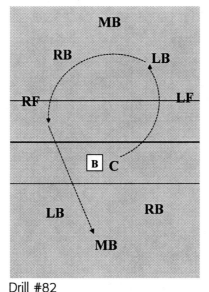

Drill #82

9

Team-Defense Drills

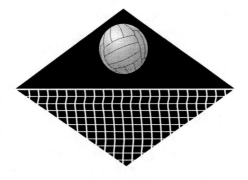

Drill #83: Team Defense to 18 Points

Objective: To learn to stuff block the ball or dig, transition, and hit a quick out of the middle

Set-up: All players; a supply of volleyballs; a scoreboard

Description: The drill involves positioning one team of six on one side of the court to play team defense. The other side has a setter in the front row and several players passing and hitting. Extra players fill in the back row to pass and play defense. The drill starts with a player in the back row for the team of six serving the ball over the net. The team of six then plays defense against the setter and two front-row hitters. They earn a point if they can stuff block the ball or if they dig the ball and transition successfully with a quickset to the middle hitter. The coach establishes a system (e.g., a scorecard or scoreboard) to keep track of points earned. The drill continues until the team playing defense scores three points, either by blocking the ball or digging and transitioning out of the middle. When that team scores three points, they then switch front-row and back-row players and make any necessary substitutions.

Coaching Point: This drill is a good exercise to get the setter to start setting the middle in transition. It will be up to the coach if she lets the players start forcing it at first and maybe making some poor sets. On the other hand, they must train like this to get better and see that digs off the net can still be set to the middle. The coach should keep an eye on the middles, since they may tire if the team cannot play very good defense. Every effort must be undertaken to make sure they stay safe in their movements.

Variations: This drill can require a much higher number of successful repetitions to be performed. On the other hand, coaches want to make sure that their middles stay sharp. Back row hitters can be added.

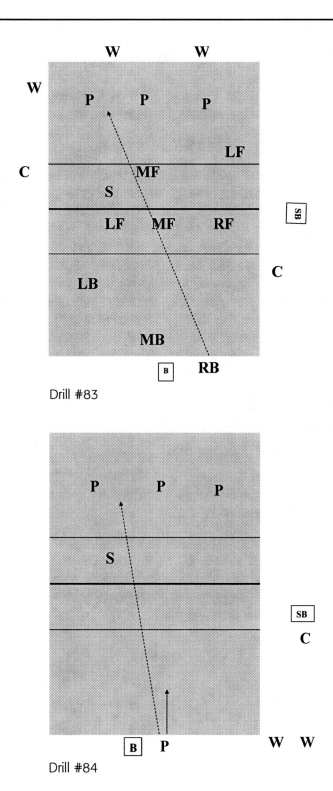

Drill #83

Drill #84

Drill #84: Add-On Defense

Objective: To help players learn to appreciate their teammates and to see how the team should be able to touch every ball the opponent hits over the net

Set-up: All players; a supply of volleyballs; a scoreboard

Description: The drill involves having one player start on the defensive side of the court against a passer, several attackers, and a setter on the other side of the court. To start the drill, the defensive player serves the ball over the net to the passer, who then passes the ball to the setter. The setter then sets one of the hitters on her side of the net. The server moves into the court to play defense. She does her best to read the pass, read the setter, and then read the hitter and attempt to dig the ball to the target or at least touch the ball. The player gets a point if she touches the ball, no matter where it goes after that. Once the player touches three balls, she is finished, and another player comes out on the court to attempt to touch three balls. Once all the players have been through this rotation, it starts again, with two players out on the court trying to touch three balls before getting out of the drill. After everyone has gone through the drill with a partner, a group of three players goes out on the court and attempts to touch three balls that are attacked over the net. Then, groups of four players go through the drill, then five players, and then finally a group of six players or a full team sees how long it takes them to touch three balls.

Coaching Point: This drill is designed to demonstrate to the players that there should never be a time when a ball is attacked over the net, and it goes untouched. The drill also helps them learn to respect their teammate's space and to see how well the court can be covered by six people.

Variations: The drill can also be done in reverse by starting with six players on the court and removing one player at a time, until only one person is left to play defense. A system for reducing the number of players participating in the drill might be situation driven, for example, when a player makes an error on defense, she has to step off the court until all of the players are off the court.

Drill #85: Attacking Overpasses

Objective: To help blockers learn the position and timing necessary to hit a ball passed or dug over the net

Set-up: Six players; a supply of volleyballs

Description: The drill involves having three players start at the net in their blocking positions along the net. A player who is positioned across the net at least 15 feet deep (or deeper) starts the drill by tossing a volleyball up so that it drops just on top of the net or on the other side in front of the blocker. The blocker then jumps up and attacks the ball back at an angle into the court. Each blocker should score on five tossed balls before switching with her partner. Each player should work at the position along the net where she normally plays in the front row (e.g., the left side, the middle, or the right side), so she can learn the angles she needs to hit the ball to keep it in the court to score.

Coaching Point: Each player should learn the timing required concerning when to jump and attack the ball, based on the trajectory of the pass coming back toward the net. The tossing height and speed should be varied, as well as the position along the net, in order to make the blocker have to adjust to the approaching ball in front of their hitting shoulder. Coaches and players should be careful to watch for loose volleyballs under the net before a ball is tossed.

Variations: A player could be positioned in front of the blocker to try to block her hit or to joust with her to try to push the ball to land in the opponent's court or off her hands out of bounds.

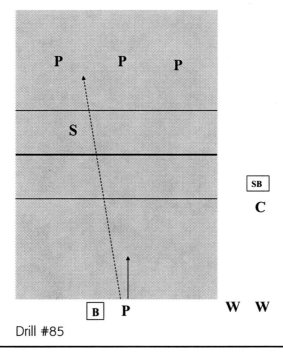

Drill #85

10

Transition Drills

Drill #86: Three-Deep with Setters and Middles

Objective: To give players experience hitting out of the back row and playing defense against a setter, a middle hitter, and a back-row attacker

Set-up: All players; a supply of volleyballs

Description: The players should divide up evenly on both sides of the net, with a setter and a middle hitter on each side. The drill starts with three players in the back row for each side, with a setter in the front row. One of the players serves the ball, and the receiving team passes the ball to the setter and prepares to be set for a back-row attack. The setter has the option to dump or tip the ball over the net instead of setting it to an attacker. The serving team should be in their base position, ready for the setter to dump the ball over. As soon as they see the setter set the back-row attacker, they call "down ball" and back up to their down-ball positions along the endline. Back-row players can rotate off the court and let others come in after every rally (or every three rallies) to keep everyone involved. As soon as possible, the middle hitters can be added to the drill. At that point, the receiving team can pass, set (dump), or set the middle. The defense must stay in their base position for a setter dump, a quick set to the middle, or a set to one of the back-row attackers. The opposing middle should attempt to block the ball and then transition off the net to attack a quick set.

Coaching Point: This drill is an excellent exercise to get the defense playing base and then to back up to dig a back-row attack. Teams tend to love this drill because everyone gets an opportunity to hit. As a rule, the drill becomes very competitive. The coach should be ready to play a ball in after an error, so the player gets an immediate opportunity to experience success.

Variations: This drill can be run with just three players on each side, with one of them setting the ball to another back-row player. Next, setters can be added to the drill and then the middles to make it an action-packed endeavor involving serving, passing, setting, hitting, blocking, and digging.

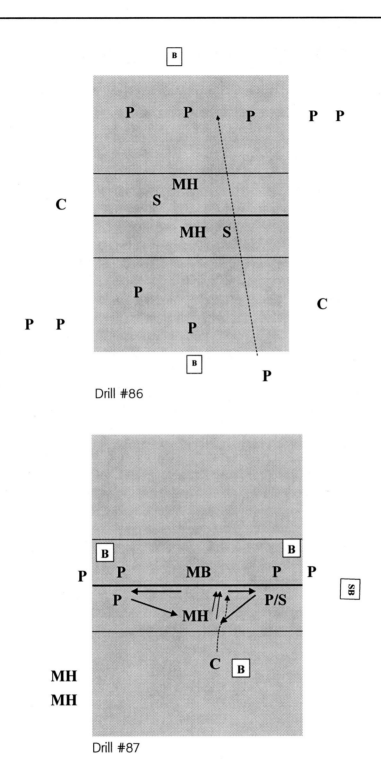

Drill #86

Drill #87

Drill #87: Middle Hitter Transition

Objective: To train middle hitters to hit a quick set, take the proper blocking steps to their outside blocker, and then quickly transition off the net to hit another set

Set-up: Seven players; three baskets of volleyballs

Description: The drill involves positioning a middle blocker and two players on one side of the net on the outside, each with a basket of volleyballs. The other side of the net has a middle hitter, two outside blockers, and a setter in the back row. The setter could also be in right front as one of the blockers. The coach is behind the attack line with a basket of volleyballs. The middle hitter begins at the attack line. To start the drill, the coach tosses the ball to the setter. The hitter follows it in and hits a quick set around the middle blocker. She then moves to the left to block a ball that will be tossed and attacked by the player on the other side of the net. The middle attempts to block that ball down into the opponent's court with her partner. The middle hitter then turns and transitions quickly off the net, getting back to the middle of the court and near the attack line so she can follow the next toss to the setter and attack that ball. She then immediately moves to the right to block a ball on that side of the court with her partner and transitions off the net attack to attack the volleyball tossed to the setter by the coach. The hitter should be given a certain number of good attacks and good blocks to achieve to end the drill. Initially, the drill should start with requiring relatively low numbers, such as three good hits and three good blocks.

Coaching Point: It is important for the coach to control the speed of this drill. The drill should be performed very slowly when the players are learning it. It is also important to watch for undue fatigue, since the players tend to tire very quickly. The drill should be stopped when/if the middle hitter begins to lose control of her steps. This drill depletes the energy system very quickly. Middles have referred to it as the "blue-lip" drill, since their lips sometimes turn blue as they go through it. All the balls should be picked up and kept off the court.

Variations: The coach should make sure to toss the ball from both sides of the court so the middle has to look over her left or right shoulder and then follow the ball in to the setter.

Drill #88: Transition Offense

Objective: To help players learn to transition from defense to offense

Set-up: All players; a supply of volleyballs

Description: The drill involves one court with six players in their defensive positions, playing against three attackers and a setter on the other side. A ball is served into the offensive side of the net. One of the players passes the volleyball to the setter, who can either dump the ball or set it to one of the attackers in the front row or back row. The team playing defense must dig the ball up and score on offense immediately. They must do this two times in a row to rotate. Blocking a ball counts as half a point. The defensive team must get two points in a row to rotate.

Coaching Point: This drill is designed to increase the pressure to play great defense and then to translate that pressure into points immediately, without going into a long rally. Starting the drill with a serve and a pass enables the defense to read both the pass and the setter and to enhance their opportunity to be successful.

Variations: This drill could involve just playing defense against back-row attackers and the setter. The scoring could vary as well, with only one point needed or three points in a row, depending on the skill level of the team.

Drill #89: Coverage Offense

Objective: To train players to be ready to transition and attack after they dig a ball up

Set-up: Eight players; a supply of volleyballs

Description: This drill begins by having a double block in front of an attacker. The attacker has a full team surrounding her. The attacker "intentionally" hits the ball into the block. The players covering the player dig it up and back out or move to a position along the net to become an attacker.

Coaching Point: This drill is designed to increase the confidence of the hitter by knowing that her teammates are backing her up and that the team can keep the ball in play and swing again for another point.

Variations: A coach or player may replace the blockers and just toss a ball back into the court after the player spikes the ball. The coach or player can vary the direction and trajectory of the ball "being blocked."

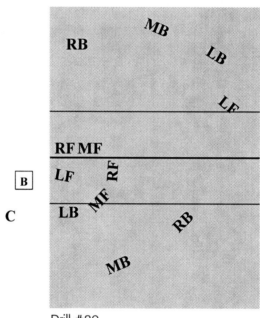

Drill #89

Drill #90: Attackers vs. the Wall

Objective: To teach players how to hit off a blocker's hand and how to use the sideline

Set-up: Six players; a supply of volleyballs; a wall (flat surface); floor tape

Description: The drill involves putting a piece of tape up on the wall at the height of the net and a piece of tape up on the wall for each antenna. The floor should also be marked with tape showing the outline of the court. Six players are positioned inside the outlined court, facing the wall where the net would be. A ball is tossed into the team, who then pass, set, and spike it against the wall over the net-height line and inside the antenna. The rest of the players cover and dig up the ball if it comes back inside the marked court. They dig it up, set it, and attack it against the wall again. The attacker learns how to hit the ball, keeping it in front of her hitting shoulder and to hit the ball so that it hits the wall (or blocker) and deflect off the wall and land outside the marked sideline. It is important that the left-side and right-side hitters learn how to "tool" or hit off the blocker's hands.

Coaching Point: The coach should make sure the players do not touch the wall (net) at any time. The setter should keep the ball off the wall (net) so the hitter can take a full swing at the ball, just like on a regular court with a net.

Variations: The ball can be introduced by being thrown into the wall so it will come back into the court, with the team in coverage position.

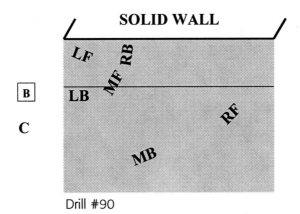

Drill #90

11

Six-on-Six Drills

Drill #91: Ball-Control Tip Scrimmage

Objective: To improve the accuracy of digging or passing a slow-moving ball

Set-up: All players; a supply of volleyballs

Description: One team starts in their team defense, while the other team is on offense. The drill begins when a ball is sent over the net to the team beginning on offense. That team passes the ball up to the setter. If it is a good pass, the setter sets the ball to one of the team's hitters, who tips the ball over the net. The other team then passes the ball up to their setter. The setter sets the ball to one of her team's hitters, and the drill continues. The coach should stop the drill if the pass is not made precisely to the setter. The drill starts over if it is not perfect. The drill involves having the teams try to get the ball across the net a certain number of times, starting with a low number, such as three to five.

Coaching Point: It may take the players a little while to develop the necessary control during this drill. They should be patient, while they learn to pass a tipped ball exactly to the setter from various positions on the court.

Variations: Once the teams can get the ball to their setter perfectly, then another component can be added to the drill. For example, the drill can require the attacker to have a perfect approach and timing to hit the ball. If it is a poor set and the attacker cannot get a perfect approach with the ball in front of her hitting shoulder, the drill should stop and start back at zero. Once the team has exhibited the skill necessary to make a perfect pass and perfect approaches, the concept of everyone covering their hitter could then be added to the drill. Collectively, this scenario typically takes a while to get all the players trained to pass perfectly, set perfectly, and then cover everyone properly.

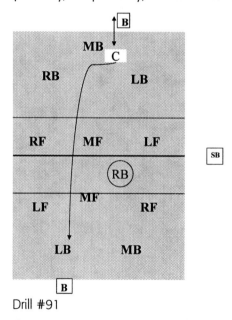

Drill #91

Drill #92: Front Row vs. Front Row

Objective: To train top players against each other at the net

Set-up: All players; a supply of volleyballs

Description: The drill involves having the starters or top team all start at a position in the front row along the net. The drill can be run as a scrimmage. The only difference in this scrimmage is the top team rotates around the net. For example, when the right side is ready to rotate to the back row, they exchange places with the right side on the other side of the net. The back row for both teams is made up of the second string or non-starters. They rotate from one team to another, staying in the back row.

Coaching Point: This drill is designed to give the stronger players an opportunity to attack and block against the strongest players on their team, while still scrimmaging. It is a good way to mix the teams up, while still challenging everyone.

Variations: The drill can be changed to have the second string or non-starters play at the net and the starters stay in the back row.

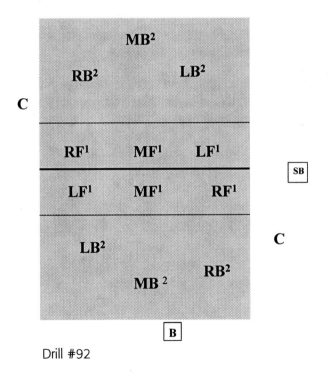

Drill #92

Drill #93: Invisible Volleyball

Objective: To help players learn to "read" their opponent's actions

Set-up: All players; no volleyballs

Description: This drill involves conducting a scrimmage, without using a volleyball. One team gets to serve first. The receiving team "reads" the server to see where the ball is being served. The person receiving the imaginary ball then passes it to the setter or target area. The setter then "reads" the passer and moves to set the ball. The attackers "read" the setter to see which hitter is being set. The hitter then hits the ball against the defense. The defenders "read" the hitter and attempt to block the ball or dig it if it goes by the block. Play continues if the ball is dug up to the setter. The ball is then set and attacked.

Coaching Point: This drill could actually be called "ideal volleyball," because the players' technique should be perfect with no ball to adjust to. This exercise is a fun drill to do with the team, because everyone is moving like they are passing the serve, the setter will be off balance setting, and the hitter or blocker will be in the net. It is important to remember that no ball is being used in the drill. Unfortunately, much of the players' movement is habitual without any regard for the volleyball, which the drill ably points out to the coach. It also shows the coach that no one ever thinks they have scored. They just continue to play until the coach stops the play.

Variations: A volleyball can be added to the drill to increase the level of action. Using a volleyball should now help players better read the opponents and anticipate where the ball will go, based on what they "see and read."

Drill #94: Six-vs.-Six Situation Drills

Objective: To train the team to compete to win in different situations

Set-up: All players; a supply of volleyballs; index cards with situations and consequences written on them

Description: The drill involves setting up two teams on the court. A representative from one team comes over and "blindly" selects one of the drills on various index cards that the coach has written up. The situation detailed on the cards includes the score for each team, with the starting team beginning with fewer points. The scores are set so winning the game will end at a natural game ending (25 points, 30 points, or 15 points). The card also gives the focus of that particular game, such as both teams can only earn points when the setter dumps the ball or the middle scores on a hit. Other situations for games may include double points for the second team when they score and only single points for the starting team. At the conclusion of the game, the losing team sends a player over to select an index card with a consequence on it for her team to do. Potential consequences may include performing certain physical activities, such as one minute of push-ups or sit-ups, a 90-second wall sit, lunges done the length of the court and back, two minutes of jumping rope, two sprints the length of the court, etc.

Coaching Point: The consequences are intended to make the losing team push a little harder to win the next time. The players determine their own consequence from the stack of cards by selecting one of them without knowing which one they will draw. All factors considered, the consequences should not involve harsh punishments. The coach should do a good job of setting up the scoring, so that both teams have an opportunity to win. A different situation for each practice can be prescribed, depending on what the team needs to improve upon in actual match situations.

Variations: The coach can change the situations and consequences each time a game during this drill ends.

Drill #95: Side-Out Scoring

Objective: To increase the focus of the team on the importance of scoring when their team is serving

Set-up: All players; a supply of volleyballs; a scoreboard

Description: This drill is set up as a regular scrimmage, with six players on each side of the court. The only way a team can score a point is if their team served the ball. The drill ends when the first team gets to 15 points.

Coaching Point: This drill is a good activity on which to keep statistics on players, such as passing, hitting percentage, "hittable" sets, digs, service aces, etc.

Variations: The score of the game can be set at different points. For example, the scoreboard can start with both teams having zero points or both teams having 15 points. The drill can mandate that the teams have to play to 25 or 30 points, scoring only when their team serves. The starting score can be different for both teams, in order to provide more of a challenge to a starting team.

Drill #96: Wash Drill With a Free Ball

Objective: To train players how to win two rallies in a row

Set-up: All players; a supply of volleyballs; a scoreboard

Description: The teams are set up for a six-on-six scrimmage. The drill begins when one team serves the ball. The teams then play it out, until one team wins the rally. The winning team immediately has a free ball sent into the court by the coach or a player not in the drill. The winning team has to score on that free ball. If they score on that rally, they get a point. If they do not score on that free ball, the situation is called a "wash" because both teams won a rally. No points are given. The team that wins the free-ball rally gets to serve. The team that wins that rally gets to receive a free ball. If that team wins the free-ball rally, they score a point. Either team gets to rotate when they get two points. The team that rotates around the court first wins the game.

Coaching Point: This drill is a good exercise to work on teams learning to be consistent in winning back-to-back rallies. The drill moves at a fairly fast pace to keep the players communicating about what is happening next. It is also a great drill to work on various free-ball plays.

Variations: This drill could become even tougher by making a team win the first rally and then two different free-ball rallies to score three times in a row to get one point. The drill may require that the two free balls have to be different plays in order for a team to win.

Drill #97: Wash Drill With a Down Ball

Objective: To train players how to win two rallies in a row

Set-up: All players; a supply of volleyballs; a scoreboard

Description: The drill involves having the teams set up for a six-on-six scrimmage. To begin the drill, one team serves the ball. The teams then play it out until one team wins the rally. The winning team immediately has a down ball (a standing back-row attack) sent into the court by the coach or a player. If they score on that down ball, they get a point. If they do not score on that down ball, it is called a "wash" because both teams won a rally. No points are given. The team that wins the down-ball rally gets to serve. The team that wins that rally gets to receive a down ball. If that team wins the down-ball rally, they score a point. Either team gets to rotate when they get two points. The team that rotates around the court first wins the game.

Coaching Point: This drill is a good exercise to work on teams learning to be consistent in winning back-to-back rallies. The drill moves at a fairly fast pace to keep the players communicating with each other about what is happening next. It is also a great drill to work on playing defense against a back-row attack.

Variations: This drill could become even tougher by making a team win the first rally and then win both a free-ball rally and a down-ball rally to score three times in a row to get one point.

Drill #98: Competing for Objects

Objective: To reward players for winning competition

Set-up: All players; a supply of volleyballs; items to given to the winning team

Description: The drill involves having teams play a regular scrimmage. When a team wins the rally, one player runs over to the sideline, picks up an item, and places it on her team's sideline near the bench. The game goes on, with the objects going back and forth until all the items end up with one team.

Coaching Point: This drill is a fun activity for the players. The objects can be items such as candy bars, drinks, pizza boxes, new items of clothing (t-shirts, socks, etc.), etc. Players tend to get really excited when they see what they can win. Relatively speaking, they tend to work hard to get those items, as opposed to winning points on a scoreboard.

Variations: This drill can be adapted in a variety of ways by changing the prizes to coupons to use on various things, such as only practice an hour, don't have to carry equipment, the winning team doesn't have to shag balls the next day in practice, etc. The coach should be creative and determine what best motivates her players.

Drill #98

Drill #99: Roll the Dice Secret Scoring

Objective: To have teams learn to work hard for every point

Set-up: All players; a supply of volleyballs; a pair of dice

Description: The drill involves setting the teams up to play six-vs.-six. One person from each team rolls one die to see how many points (one through six) her team needs to score before the other team gets to their number of points. The opposing team does not know how many points their opponent needs. The scrimmage is run like a regular game, with one team winning when they get to the number of points that was rolled on their die. There is a slight consequence for the losing team (e.g., perform calisthenics, run sprints, etc.).

Coaching Point: This drill is designed to bring high energy to each rally, since the players are not sure how many points their opponents need to beat them. It could be just one point, six points, or any number in between.

Variations: The coach can have the teams keep playing after one team wins to see if the other team can win on the total number of points on both dice to keep from doing their consequence activity. The coach could also use more than one die for each team, thereby increasing the number of points needed to win.

Drill #100: Bonus Ball

Objective: To check the intensity of the team when winning a rally, with the bonus ball counting as five points

Set-up: All players; a supply of volleyballs; one different colored volleyball; a scoreboard

Description: The drill involves setting the players up for a six-on-six scrimmage. The teams play a normal scoring game until the coach throws in a bonus ball (a different colored ball). The team that wins the rally with the bonus ball scores five points.

Coaching Point: The bonus ball can be thrown in to either side to help boost the team that needs the extra points to keep the score close.

Variations: The ball could be used at regular intervals in the scrimmage, such as every time a team reaches a score that is a multiple of five.

Drill #101: Score Switch

Objective: To help players continue to play hard, regardless of whether they are winning or losing

Set-up: All players; a supply of volleyballs; a scoreboard

Description: The drill involves setting the players up for a six-on-six scrimmage. The teams compete against one another with regular scoring. The drill includes the feature of allowing the coach to walk over to the scoreboard and switch the scores of the teams at any time. The game continues until one team wins.

Coaching Point: This drill is designed to keep both teams playing hard to score points, no matter what the scoreboard shows.

Variations: The score could automatically be switched every five minutes until one team wins.

About the Author

Dr. Cecile Reynaud is a faculty member in the sport management program at Florida State University. Previously, she served as the head women's volleyball coach at FSU from 1976 to 2001, compiling 636 career wins. In the process, Reynaud led the Seminoles to six conference championships and was named conference coach of the year four times. She was an assistant coach with the USA World University Games team in 1983 and the head coach of the Junior National team in 1985. Reynaud also served as an interim assistant athletic director at FSU and senior women's administrator from 1994-95, where she was responsible for 13 sports. She completed her doctorate in sport management in 1998.

Dr. Reynaud was selected as the 1996 USA Volleyball George J. Fischer Leader in Volleyball Award recipient. She is a former member of the USA Volleyball board of directors and a past executive committee member. She continues to serve as a USA Volleyball Coaching Accreditation Program (CAP) instructor. From 1986-1994, she was an administrator in the Olympic Festivals. She served as the technical secretary for the men's and women's volleyball competition at the Goodwill Games in 1990.

She is co-editor of the *Volleyball Coaching Bible* and also the editor of *She Can Coach!* She has also produced a well-received instructional DVD series on volleyball for Coaches Choice. She has served as a television color analyst for collegiate volleyball matches and participated in the 1996 Olympic Games in Atlanta as volleyball's deputy competition manager. She also speaks annually at the NCAA Women Coaches Academy and the NACWAA summer institutes.

In 1989 and 1990, she served two years as president of the American Volleyball Coaches Association (AVCA), after serving a two-year term as the awards chair in 1986 and 1987. She currently serves on the AVCA board of directors as the education and publications chair. She presents annually at the AVCA convention, as well as serving as emcee of the AVCA Coach of the Year Banquet and the AVCA All-America/Players of the Year Banquet. She is also a member of the *International Journal of Volleyball Research* review board.

She graduated from Webster Groves (MO) High School and was inducted into their Athletic Hall of Fame in 2006. She attended Southwest Missouri State University in Springfield, MO, where she played field hockey and volleyball. She was inducted into the SMSU Athletic Hall of Fame in 1983. Following graduation in 1975, she taught physical education and health in Steelville, MO for one year and coached girl's volleyball, basketball, softball, and track for the high school. She earned her master's degree at Florida State University in 1978, while serving as the head women's volleyball coach.

Dr. Reynaud is on the Refuge House board of directors, a local domestic and sexual abuse shelter, an organization which she served as president for two years.